Wicked Newport

Wicked Newport

SORDID STORIES FROM THE CITY BY THE SEA

Larry Stanford

Illustrations by J. Bailey

THE
History
PRESS

Published by The History Press
Charleston, SC 29403
www.historypress.net

Copyright © 2008 by Larry Stanford
All rights reserved

Cover design by Marshall Hudson.

First published 2008
Second printing 2009
Third printing 2010
Fourth printing 2010
Fifth printing 2011
Sixth printing 2011
Seventh printing 2012

ISBN 978.1.5402.1812.4

Library of Congress Cataloging-in-Publication Data

Stanford, Larry.
Wicked Newport : sordid stories from the city by the sea / Larry Stanford.
p. cm.
Includes bibliographical references.
ISBN 978-1-5402-1812-4
1. Newport (R.I.)--History--Anecdotes. 2. Newport (R.I.)--Biography--Anecdotes. 3.
Scandals--Rhode Island--Newport--History--Anecdotes. 4. Corruption--Rhode Island--
Newport--History--Anecdotes. 5. Newport (R.I.)--Social life and customs--Anecdotes. I.
Title.
F89.N5S69 2008
974.5'7--dc22
2008014320

contents

ACKNOWLEDGEMENTS

I would like to thank the folks at The History Press for all their help and support in getting *Wicked Newport* published.

Thanks also go to my colleagues and mentors at the Newport, Rhode Island Convention and Visitors Bureau, especially President Evan Smith. His passion for tourism and Newport history is infectious and an inspiration to everyone he comes in contact with. Also, a thank-you to Kathryn Farrington, Cathy Morrison and their staffs at the CVB for their dedication to delivering a wonderful experience to everyone who visits "the City by the Sea."

A very special thanks goes to Jennifer Bailey for her time and effort for adding her artistic touches to the original sketches seen throughout this book.

Without the inspiration of history teacher extraordinaire Charlie Ryan, this book would not have been possible. Thanks for making history fun and interesting to learn.

I would also be remiss if I did not acknowledge Key West author David Sloan. For your friendship and hospitality, I am grateful.

A special thanks also goes out to the professor Thomas Cornell XV for his assistance in locating the lost graves of his ancestors.

I am also grateful to the queen of Newport retail, Lisa, and her crew at Only in Rhode Island. Thanks for the front-row positioning of *Wicked Newport*.

Last but not least, I must thank my Facebook Angels, Rachel, Tess, Katie J. and Kathleen. Because of you, I have the most attractive friends of anyone online. You have truly inspired me to take my writing to the next level. Thank you!

introduction

Newport, Rhode Island, represents a variety of things to a multitude of people. For over a million guests annually, the city symbolizes a picturesque getaway with priceless mansions, unforgettable harbor tours or a meal at a waterfront eatery. To many natives, Newport is the town where they were born and has been the only place they have ever lived. Those who are old enough have seen their city evolve from a strategic navy port to a tourist mecca. For those of us who have made Newport our adopted hometown, it represents a place with unique architecture, stunning ocean views and perhaps a small taste of what colonial life was like.

Newport has certainly come a long way from its infancy as a tiny enclave of pioneers seeking their religious freedom in 1639. The city progressed into a thriving colonial seaport, then subsequently an encampment for British soldiers; a depressed fishing village; a summer getaway for wealthy Southern planters; a colony for artists, writers and intellectuals; the playground for America's super wealthy; a strategic navy base; and eventually a world-renowned resort area. Who knows what the city will evolve into next? The best part of all these diverse layers of history is that there is at least a small remnant of each era still in existence in Newport to this day.

One thing you will notice as you progress through your reading is the frequent number of times New York City and Newport are linked. Throughout Newport's gilded era, it would be almost impossible to mention one location without the other. These two cities will be inexorably linked throughout history because of the steady stream of affluent globetrotters who spent at least a portion of the summer season seaside. Many of the characters highlighted in this book may have earned their vast fortunes in New York, but chose Newport to spend their seemingly unending flow of capital in an attempt to out-build, out-spend and out-entertain each other. "The City that Never Sleeps" and "The City by the Sea" have seen their fair share of these people's indiscretions and we are more than happy to share some of the more memorable ones with you in the next few chapters.

Hopefully, you will have as much fun reading about these unsolved mysteries, colorful characters and salacious scandals as I have had writing about them. Enjoy!

THE MYSTERY TOWER

Atop one of the highest points in all the city of Newport, Rhode Island, stands an object that has been perhaps the most controversial structure in all of the Americas. The first time one sees the mysterious structure, one cannot help but be awed by the size and symmetry of this beautifully constructed circular stone tower. After looking over the object, the mind drifts to its purpose and to the obvious question of why this thing was built.

Unfortunately, there is no easy or concrete answer. Philosophers, scientists, theologians and just about every man, woman and child who lay eyes on it come to their own conclusions. Locals and visitors alike have been trying to solve this mystery for over three hundred years. One thing is for sure—it was built by someone and must have served a specific purpose. There seem to be more questions than answers when it comes to the Mystery Tower.

Let's examine the few known facts we do have about the tower. It is defiantly circular and constructed of local, mostly flat stones set in mortar to hold the stones stable and in place. For the structure's support, there are eight arched columns of flat stone. Each arch measures seven and a half feet in height. The curved portion of each arch contains flat stones angled toward the ground, also held in place by mortar. Above the arches is the main body of the tower. A look inside the circular portion reveals notches in the stones where crossbeams may have held up a floor at one time. There are also three small, square windows, with one facing Newport harbor. Curiously, there is an indentation on the inside wall that seems to have been a fireplace. The total height of the tower is twenty-four feet with the width across at twenty-three feet. That's where the absolutes end and the theories begin, with some more plausible than others. Let's examine some of the most popular theories that have evolved over the years.

The most romanticized of all the tower's possible builders is the Viking or Norse theory. It is so prevalent in Newport's popular culture that

Newport's Old Stone Mill remains one of our country's great unsolved architectural mysteries. The mysterious tower sits atop one of the tallest hills in Newport and its actual purpose for construction is still unknown. *Photo courtesy of the author.*

many local businesses, including a luxury hotel and a tour company, use the name "Viking." Even the local high school uses the nickname "the Vikings." The origin of this hypothesis came from a Danish scholar named Carl Christian Rafn, who published a series of letters called the *Antiquitates Americanae* in 1837. Rafn drew the conclusion that Viking explorers visited the area and built the tower as a house of worship in the early eleventh century. He based his assumption on some poorly drawn architectural drawings of similar structures. Later, scholars also ran with these ideas to make their arguments that the tower was of Viking origin. There is evidence that Norse explorers visited Mount Hope Bay in Rhode Island between AD 1000 and 1004. Another argument these theorists use is that the tower's construction is similar to early church buildings in northern Europe. One major point that proponents of this theory argue is that the Newport tower is oriented to true points of the compass, just like early stone churches in Norway and Denmark. It has also been proven that Vikings did explore other parts of the North American continent.

Artifacts have been uncovered in L'Anse aux Meadows on the island of Newfoundland, in Canada. There have been numerous archaeological digs in this area, including around the tower site, yet no eleventh-century artifacts have been uncovered this far south.

Another less popular theory is that Portuguese explorers constructed the tower in the early 1500s. The Portuguese were some of the most renowned seamen in the world at this time and were credited with numerous discoveries in the New World. Prince Henry the Navigator funded dozens of expeditions along the African coast and, in 1500, Pedro Cabral claimed Brazil for his home country. The explorer who may have built the tower was Miguel Corte-Real, who disappeared off the North Atlantic around 1502. He was searching for his brother Gaspar who had been searching for the Northwest Passage. Gaspar had reached Newfoundland and then sailed southwest along the present United States coast. Gaspar was thought to have been lost in a storm somewhere off what is now the coast of New England. Miguel is thought to have sailed extensively around Narragansett Bay, before becoming wrecked himself. The tower may have been built as a signaling device or a beacon to alert possible rescuers. There is an indentation in the upper structure that looks like a fireplace, lending support to the theory that the platform could be used for a signal fire. There is also evidence of Portuguese explorers landing at Dighton Rock, in nearby Massachusetts, around 1511. A cannon and sword of Portuguese origin have also been uncovered at Fort Ninigret in Charlestown, Rhode Island. Perhaps other expeditions came to search for the lost Corte-Real brothers. No Portuguese artifacts have been located in and around Newport itself, but similar structures used as watch towers and fortified churches do exist along the Portuguese coast.

The most bizarre of the other theories is that a Chinese navigator named Zheng He built it as a lighthouse in 1421. This theory is presented in the book *1421: The Year China Discovered America*. The author argues the tower's dimensions match several measurement units used in Ming Dynasty China. He also claims that the mortar used to hold the stones together is made of crushed shells, which would be consistent with Chinese building methods. He also suggests the tower's construction was for a colony of Chinese sailors and concubines from the junks of the Zheng He voyages. Some European explorers, including Giovanni Verrazzano, described some of the natives as having skin "the color of brass" and having long, black hair. Verrazzano also noted they wore jewelry similar to people of the Far East. The lighthouse would have been used to guide future Chinese expeditions to the exact location of the colony. This tower also matches designs used in lighthouses and observatories located along the Chinese coast.

The indentation in the stonework looks similar to a modern fireplace. This would suggest a fire was needed for warmth or for use as a signaling device. *Photo courtesy of the author.*

One thing Verrazzano fails to mention in his detailed writings when he sailed through Narragansett Bay and around Newport harbor was the existence of a large stone tower. That factor, as well as a few other details, may lead to the actual builder. It is widely speculated that the first colonial governor of Rhode Island, a man named Benedict Arnold, had the tower constructed to function as a windmill. Arnold, the great-grandfather of the Revolutionary War traitor, owned large tracts of land in Newport, including the plot where the tower is located. There is evidence that a wooden windmill located on the same spot was blown down in a hurricane in 1675. There is also a similar stone windmill near Arnold's boyhood home in Chesterton, England. He also mentions "my stone built windmill" twice in his will. Arnold's Newport home was located right down the hill on Spring Street. Scientific evidence points toward seventeenth-century construction as well. An extensive archaeological dig in 1949 yielded twenty thousand artifacts, including a rusty meat cleaver, bits of a clay pipe and some coins. Also found were grinding stones, which seem to imply that the tower was actually a mill to grind grains. Studies have also analyzed the mortar holding the stones in place and it was found to be "identical in quality and character" to mortar used in construction of other seventeenth-century properties.

Perhaps we will never be sure of the actual builders. One thing is for sure—there are over one million pounds of fieldstone expertly piled to form a beautifully constructed masterpiece. If you visit Newport, it is certainly worth the trip up the hill on either Mill or Pelham Streets to Touro Park to view the tower for yourself and come up with your own theory. The mystery may never be solved, but rest assured, there are plenty of people in Newport who would like to keep it that way.

ΙΠΠΟΣΕΠΤ?

Portsmouth, Rhode Island, is a small town today. It is a nice place to raise a family: rural, picturesque and it still has a colonial feel that harkens back to the town's founding in 1638. Portsmouth also has something that many small New England towns can relate to—almost everyone knows everyone else. Keep in mind many of these families have lived in this area for hundreds of years and personal business and rumors spread quickly by word of mouth. Now imagine Portsmouth in 1673, when only a handful of newly immigrated families lived in this town; everyone *really* knows everyone else's business. This was also an era when the supernatural and invisible world played a large part in the daily lives and religious practices of the people. It was a recipe for disaster.

Those things didn't seem to matter to Thomas Cornell, a hardworking local farmer. He was too busy chopping wood, milking cows and tending to his large flock of sheep. Cornell needed to work hard; he had a lot of mouths to feed. Besides four sons from an earlier marriage, he had a new wife Sarah, their two daughters and a third on the way. Thomas had to work hard because his large family depended on him. Don't misunderstand; by all accounts, the Cornells lived fairly well. They lived in a large two-story colonial house off of West Road (now known as West Main Road) on a one-hundred-acre land grant that his father had secured from the city of Portsmouth over a quarter of a century earlier. The fairly large land grant swept west all the way down to Narragansett Bay. For a forty-six-year-old colonial farmer, he was doing pretty well for himself, at least to the outside world. There was one small catch: Thomas Cornell was not yet the owner of this farm; his widowed mother was. To make things even more complicated, Mrs. Rebecca Cornell still lived in the house with Thomas's large family. There were grumblings and rumors in the small community that tension was growing inside the home. The seventy-three-year-old matriarch of the

Cornell clan confided in some family friends that she thought she would be done away with before the year's end. There were other rumors of parental abuse and elder mistreatment, although no concrete evidence was ever substantiated. Perhaps it was just small-town gossip; or was it?

No matter what the relationship was between Thomas and his mother, the events of February 8, 1673, would change the Cornell family forever. It was a typical, cold winter day and snow blanketed the fields surrounding the homestead. Thomas returned home late in the afternoon to discover his mother was not feeling well. Upon entering the room, Thomas discovered his eldest son sitting on the bed, visiting the ailing matriarch. After Thomas's arrival, the son departed the bedroom and the pair chatted for roughly an hour and a half. It was around 7:00 p.m. That evening, when Thomas arrived at the dinner table, he announced Rebecca would not be joining the family for dinner. The elder Cornell was not fond of the evening's fare, salted fish, most likely because of its toughness. (At her advanced age, it was unlikely she had teeth.)

After dinner, Sarah sent another son, Edward, into the bedchamber to see if grandma would like some boiled milk, an item easier for her to ingest. When Edward entered the room, he made a startling discovery. There were flames dancing along the floor by the foot of the fireplace. He ran out in a panic to get a candle to illuminate the room as well as alert the others of the emergency. Everyone in the house raced to the room to investigate.

The first to arrive was Henry Straite, a boarder in the Cornell house. He saw the flames on the floor and immediately patted them down with his hands to prevent their spreading, ignoring any possible injury to himself. Straite also noticed a badly burned body on the floor, which he misidentified as "a drunken Indian." It was common at this time for local Native Americans to get drunk and commit crimes in the area. When Thomas entered the room, he knew it was no Indian. He cried out, "Oh Lord, it is my mother!" The body was burned so badly that they could only recognize Rebecca from her shoes. A servant ran to the neighbors' houses to alert them of what had occurred and many of the local town elders came to view the horrible scene. The next day the town coroner, as well as a quickly constructed panel of inquiry—including many of the town elders who had viewed the charred corpse—set off on the grizzly task of determining cause of death. After a lengthy examination, including the removal of all charred clothing, the all-layman panel determined the following: "Rebecca Cornell was brought to her untimely death by an Unhappy Accident of fire as Shee satt in her Rome." The panel concluded that Rebecca's burns and subsequent death were caused by a flaming ember from her pipe that caused her woolen clothes to catch fire and burn her around her head, shoulders and chest.

That evening, two of the town elders' wives prepared the body for burial. Sarah Cornell was curiously absent from the ritual. Was it tension between Sarah and her mother-in-law that precluded her from preparing the body, or was it the superstitions regarding pregnant women and the dead? Folklore was taken seriously at this time and it was believed a dead person could possess the unborn fetus or perhaps cause a deformity to the child. Whatever the reason, the pregnant Sarah kept her distance.

The next day, February 10, 1673, Rebecca Cornell was buried in a family plot overlooking Narragansett Bay. This burial should have marked the end of this terrible family tragedy, but the living world and the supernatural world were about to collide. Rebecca's earthly body had been laid to rest, but her spirit was alive and it had a lot to say!

Two nights later, on February 12, Rebecca Cornell's brother, John Briggs, had a surprise visitor as he slept. His bed sheets were ripped off of him by a ghostly apparition. He cried out to the spirit, "In the name of God, what art thou?" The dimly lit spirit replied, "I am your sister Cornell," then repeated twice, "See how I was burned by fire!" John Briggs would recount later that he did not recognize his older sister because she was disfigured from burns. Ghosts were taken very seriously in colonial Portsmouth. They were considered to be sent directly from God as messengers to rectify their untimely deaths and exact revenge upon their murderers. After a week of consulting with family and perhaps his clergyman, John Briggs went to the deputy governor and town council to detail his shocking late night visit. Briggs said Rebecca did not reveal her killer or if she was murdered at all and Briggs was careful not to accuse anyone of a crime. Accusing someone of murder was a serious charge and if you made the accusation, you had better be 100 percent sure of their guilt. False accusation was punishable by death. So was murdering one's parent, considered almost as heinous a crime as killing a monarch. Briggs was very persuasive in suggesting Rebecca's death may not have been accidental. The deputy governor agreed and ordered the freshly buried body exhumed for further medical examination.

This time, two Newport doctors performed the autopsy and found something previously overlooked by the panel of elders. They discovered a small puncture wound near the heart as well as bruising consistent with a blow to the chest. The doctors reported "a suspitious wound," possibly from the spindle of a spinning wheel, might have also contributed to Rebecca's death. By this time, circumstantial evidence was mounting against Thomas. Locals were coming forward with their tales of arguments between the mother and son as well as reports of threats he had made on her life. He was also the last person to see her alive. Although no murder weapon was ever located and no eyewitness saw him commit the crime, Thomas Cornell was arrested and charged with murdering Rebecca. He was thrown into a Newport jail, denied bail and made to wait for his upcoming trial.

Over three months had passed and Thomas Cornell was still in jail. Three months for prosecutors to gather evidence to present to a grand jury. Three months for rumors, hearsay and speculation to run rampant. More stories of elder abuse, hostility toward Rebecca Cornell and arguments over rent came forward to prosecutors building a case of murder. When the grand jury met on May 12, 1673, it was almost a foregone conclusion that an indictment would be handed down. Thomas was already guilty in the court of public opinion. On May 16, at Newport's White Horse Tavern, a twelve-person jury of wealthy landowners and farmers, all of whom certainly knew the Cornell family well, handed down the following verdict:

> *Whereas you* **Thomas Cornell** *have beene in this Court, Indicted, and Charged for Murdering your Mother M^{rs}* **Rebeca Cornell** *Widdow, and you being by your Peers the Jurry found Guilty, Know, and to that end, prepare your selfe, that you are by this Court sentenced to be*

The White Horse Tavern was the site of Thomas Cornell's ill-fated trial. This colonial structure still operates in the same capacity today, making it the oldest tavern building in the country. *Photo courtesy of the author.*

Miantonomi Hill was the site of Thomas Cornell's execution. The location was chosen because of its proximity to both Newport and Portsmouth. The tower currently standing on the site is a World War I memorial. *Photo courtesy of the author.*

carryed from hence to the Common Goale, and from thence on ffryday next which will be the 23ᵗʰ Day of this instant month May, about one of the Clocke, to be carryed from the sayd Goale to the place of Execution, the Gallows, and there to be Hanged by yᵉ neck untill you are Dead Dead.

With the jury's decree, which was largely based on hearsay, small-town gossip and the testimony of a ghost, Thomas was sentenced to death by hanging.

The execution took place one week later on Miantonomi Hill, which is located at the northern edge of Newport, with commanding views of Narragansett Bay to the west. This location was also a short distance from Portsmouth, so any interested parties could also be present. A fairly large crowd of a thousand townsfolk had gathered; executions were considered a public spectacle. This trial was special, with such controversy and public fanfare. On his way to the gallows, Thomas requested burial in the family plot next to his mother. His request was denied. He also never changed his story, even with the rope around his neck; Thomas Cornell professed his innocence until his last breath. Just after 1:00 p.m. on May 23, 1673, Thomas took his last breath, hanged for a crime he may not have committed.

Thomas's hanging should have put to rest this awful chapter in the Cornell family history, but that was not the case. Murder and misfortune seemed to follow the family well into the future. Another panel of inquest was convened to examine Sarah's role in the death of her mother-in-law. She was later acquitted. The third child of Thomas and Sarah Cornell was born the same year of her father's execution and defiantly named Innocent. Innocent would marry a man named Richard Borden and six generations later, in 1860, Elizabeth Borden was born in Fall River, Massachusetts. We know her better as "Lizzie."

On August 4, 1892, Lizzie's father Andrew and stepmother Abby were both brutally murdered in their Fall River home by an axe-wielding assailant. Lizzie was arrested and charged with both crimes. There was tension between father and daughter over Andrew's will as well as friction between Lizzie and her stepmother Abby. There were even rumors of a lesbian affair between Lizzie and a Boston actress named Nance O'Neil. The speculation

This is the actual evidence photo of Andrew Borden, slain inside his home in Fall River, Massachusetts, on August 4, 1892. The home is now a bed-and-breakfast and they do daily reenactments of the murders.

The infamous Lizzie Borden. Although Lizzie was the prime suspect for murdering both her father and stepmother, she was eventually found not guilty. As a direct descendant of the Cornell family, is it possible that matricide and patricide are hereditary?

was that Lizzie killed her wealthy banker father to support her struggling actress girlfriend. Because of a lack of hard evidence, especially the fact that there were no eyewitnesses and that no murder weapon was ever found, Lizzie was acquitted of all charges. These were similar circumstances to Thomas Cornell's trial, but with vastly different results.

Was the Cornell family predisposed to murdering parents or was it just an ironic twist of fate? The Cornell legacy lives on to this day. A descendant founded Cornell University in 1865. There is even a Thomas Cornell living in Newport today. He is a fifteenth-generation Rhode Islander descended from the original Thomas Cornell who received his land grant around 1646. This present-day Thomas Cornell has his own version of the events that led to his namesake's execution. He has no doubt that Rebecca Cornell died from an accidental fire ignited by her pipe. She did have a bad habit of falling asleep with her pipe still lit. Cornell also believes that by the time she woke up, she was quickly asphyxiated by the smoke and fell to the ground

Fifteenth-generation Newporter Thomas Cornell stands between headstones of his ancestors in a burial plot that was once part of the Cornell family farm. The present-day Thomas Cornell is convinced his namesake would never have been found guilty in a modern-day courtroom. *Photo courtesy of the author.*

gasping for air. This would also explain the wound to her chest. This is certainly a plausible explanation and one that did not get fully explored at trial. The sad truth is the jury ignored the results of the first inquiry, which concluded that the death was caused by a fire from the embers of Rebecca's pipe. Instead they chose to focus on the testimony of Rebecca's ghost, which, in reality, could have been a dream or even fabricated by John Briggs. This testimony certainly would not be admissible today in a modern trial. It is also doubtful Thomas had legal representation in an atmosphere of guilty-until-proven-innocent.

There is one thing we can be sure of—no modern jury would have ever convicted Thomas Cornell of matricide. With the evidence presented and the testimony given, there would have certainly been enough reasonable doubt to set him free. But Rebecca did die strangely and Thomas was a victim of his time and bizarre circumstances. Unfortunately, it was these bizarre circumstances and not his guilt that cost him his life.

THE SYMBOL OF HOSPITALITY?

You will still see Newport's symbol of colonial hospitality throughout the city today. It's the pineapple, and you will see it carved above colonial doorways as well as in souvenir shops throughout the downtown area. It was symbolic of a good voyage and a safe return after a captain had made his trip from a tropical climate. Usually a captain would display fresh pineapples on a doorway or fence post to announce his return and that his home was open to welcome visitors who wanted to pay respects and hear about his voyage to a faraway location. While its intent was hospitable and welcoming, displaying a pineapple also may have been symbolic of a dark and sinister voyage.

Newport merchants and sea captains were dependant on the sea to make their living. Newport's deep and well-protected harbor made it one of the five busiest colonial seaports, rivaling Boston, New York, Philadelphia and Charles Town (now Charleston), South Carolina, in shipping traffic. But Newport merchants and traders were at a disadvantage. Because Newport was on an island, it could not produce any of its exports without first importing the raw materials from another port. Therefore, Newport merchants became extremely wealthy acting as middlemen, purchasing goods from one local and then marking up the goods for delivery somewhere else. Essentially, many of the wealthiest Newporters during this colonial period made huge fortunes expediting goods around to the other colonies, the West Indies and even to the home country, England. Captains became experts at knowing which materials and supplies were in short supply in which port and where they could receive the highest price at market. Newport's golden age of commerce, from the 1740s right up until the American Revolution, made this city a thriving and bustling seaport with many local families making huge fortunes from this oceangoing trade.

Even if a merchant or craftsman didn't own a sailing ship during this period, it did not preclude him from cashing in on the lucrative trading

The Long Wharf area of Newport. This port was the epicenter of the city's colonial commerce. This waterfront area was one of the five busiest colonial seaports, along with Boston, New York City, Philadelphia and Charles Town, South Carolina. *Illustration by Jen Bailey.*

The pineapple is still a symbol of colonial hospitality. It was used to signify the return of a sailing vessel from a long overseas voyage. The pineapple also signified that a shipload of slaves had been delivered from Africa to a West Indian plantation. *Photo courtesy of the author.*

activity. Industries sprang up all along Newport's dock area with ship supply stores, sail-making shops and rope-makers. Other secondary markets were created as well. Barrels were in huge supply, as they were needed to export local products. There were also two local families, the Townsends and the Goddards, who were renowned throughout the colonies for their fine handcrafted furniture. Exotic wood—like mahogany, imported from the West Indies—would be combined with indigenous species like oak, maple and cherry to create some of the most beautiful dressers, desks, tables and chairs ever made. There was even a well-known local grave-carving shop owned by the Stevens family, which exported its headstones throughout New England, the Southern colonies and even Jamaica. The shop that opened in 1705 still functions as a grave-carving shop to this day. Newport's goods could be shipped to anywhere its merchant fleet traveled.

By far, the most lucrative of all eighteenth-century transactions were made during the infamous slave-based Triangle Trade. If you trace the voyage on a map, the shape of the journey looked like a triangle. Newport, at one time, had upward of fifty rum distilleries producing a liquid currency that was worth its weight in gold. Most of the time, the Newport rum would make its way all the way to the west coast of Africa, where it was exchanged for human cargo, slaves. Africa's west coast was teeming with slave-trading ports, often marked by huge castles on hillsides filled with African captives. In Africa, European traders dealt with African suppliers, seldom capturing the slaves themselves. After bartering their rum for human cargo, slave captains would sail west toward the vast sugar cane plantations of the West Indies, often unloading on the islands of Jamaica, Martinique and even Cuba. On the islands, the human cargo would be exchanged for the main ingredient in Newport rum: molasses. The captain would then return to Newport to begin the process again. Slave ship owners made many times their initial investments on these voyages and many prominent families participated in this dark exchange. It is estimated there were between twenty and thirty such ventures departing Newport at the peak of trading activity. Exact numbers cannot be determined because slave trade trips may have departed from other ports after loading supplies there or because of a captain's reluctance to declare his cargo to customs officials to avoid paying import tariffs. Newport slave captains became experts in navigating the west coast ports of Africa. Trips to Dakar in Senegal, the grain coast (which is present-day Liberia) and the cape coast (which is today in Ghana) were some of the more common stops along this Triangle Trade. It is almost humorous to think that modern-day Newport residents won't drive off the island and won't drive north the thirty minutes to Providence because it is deemed too far to travel. Yet eighteenth-century mariners sailed over five

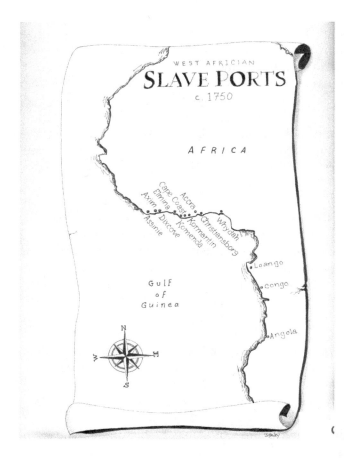

This is a map of West African slave ports. Many of these ports and fortresses were well-known to Newport captains involved in the infamous Triangle Trade. *Illustration by Jen Bailey.*

thousand miles to West Africa, and then another five thousand miles to the West Indies on the dangerous middle passage of the Triangle Trade, where they faced hurricanes and slave insurrections. These men undertook these voyages because they had no choice; they were forced to trade around the world in an attempt to make a living. There weren't enough raw materials in Newport and the surrounding areas to support the lifestyle these colonists had grown accustomed to.

These captains also became adept at acquiring a certain type of slave, depending on their final destination. For example, if the captain knew rice plantations in South Carolina were in short supply and needed an injection of field hands, he would sail first to the grain coast to pick up his slaves. These slaves, already familiar with harvesting rice in their homeland, would fetch a higher price on the rice plantation in the colonies. The captains would make a higher return on their voyage and more profit for the ship owner.

Numerous gravestones still stand that mark the final resting places of Africans brought to Newport as laborers. It was common for the slave to inherit the master's last name. *Photo courtesy of the author.*

There is no doubt that slaves taken to the sugar plantations of the Caribbean and to the rice and tobacco plantations of the South led brutal lives. After being captured by other stronger African tribes and then marched hundreds of miles to the African coast, they were kept in slave castles until sold again. Then they would be loaded onto a tiny, crowded sailing ship for a voyage of thousands of miles to reach their final destination where they could be worked to death. Not a pleasant life for sure. Many slaves died from malnutrition and illness during the long sails. As a captain and owner of a slave ship, the death only meant less profit for that voyage; it was all about earning the highest profit. One small consolation a slave might have is if the captain thought they had above-average intelligence; then, they might have been brought back to Newport for servitude. Although it was still enslavement, the captured person would certainly have a better life in Newport than almost certain death on a plantation. Many of the slaves who returned to Newport were household servants like maids and cooks. The men were taught a skill or a trade and were often rented out as skilled craftsmen to other townspeople. Some of Newport's historic colonial structures like Touro Synagogue and Redwood Library were constructed with this servant workforce. Many prominent Newport citizens owned slaves during this period, including Declaration of Independence signer William Ellery. Another exception that a slave in Newport might enjoy is the small

Violet Hammond's final resting place. It is carved prominently on the headstone that she was the wife of Cape Coast James. It was a common practice for slaves to be named after the regions of Africa where they were captured. *Photo courtesy of the author.*

possibility they could one day purchase their freedom from their owner. One such example is a cook named Duchess Quamino, who by 1780 had become a free woman through the sale of her homemade cakes. She was better known as the Pastry Queen of Rhode Island.

There are still reminders of the colonial slave trade in Newport today. As well as the previously mentioned historic buildings, many of the slave captains' and ship owners' extravagant homes still stand. There is also a section of Newport's common burying ground called "God's Little Acre." This is where Africans brought to Newport against their will were laid to rest, far from their original homelands.

The symbol of colonial hospitality undoubtedly had a different significance to different groups of people. To wealthy ship captains and slave traders, it meant a safe return and a prosperous voyage. But to enslaved Africans, the pineapple symbolized that another shipload of their brothers and sisters had been sold into slavery.

KARMA FOR THE
MERCHANT PRINCE

If you believe in karma, you subscribe to the basic premise that your actions, whether good or evil, will eventually return to affect your life. In the long run, karma will reward you if you treat others fairly and live an honest lifestyle. Karma will also eventually punish those who do not. Essentially, you reap what you sow. Apparently, Aaron Lopez did not live by this mantra. Duarte Aaron Lopez was born in Lisbon, Portugal, in 1731, to well-to-do parents. The family was forced to practice their Judaism in secret and outwardly pretend to be Roman Catholic. Aaron Lopez fled the area in 1752 to avoid further persecution from the spreading Spanish Inquisition. Lopez settled in Newport where his half brother Moses had already established a residence. Lopez, free to practice the religion of his choice in Newport, dropped "Duarte" as his first name. Aaron Lopez, with his newly found freedom of religion, set out to build a religious and business empire. He was instrumental in the building of Touro Synagogue, the oldest Jewish house of worship still standing in the United States. It was completed in 1763 for a growing Jewish population after word of mouth had spread throughout the New World that all Newporters were free to worship as they wished. This was not the case in most colonial cities. Many cities, like nearby Boston, were founded by a certain religious sect. If you lived in such a city, you were forced to practice that particular belief or face serious consequences. Newport was attracting all kinds of new religious practices in the mid-eighteenth century. Jews, Quakers and Baptists were free to concentrate their collective attention on commerce and Aaron Lopez did that better than anyone in town. He did it so well that he earned the nickname "The Merchant Prince."

Lopez had his hands in many different areas. Along with his brother Moses, he owned twenty-seven square-rigged sailing ships, which traded between the colonies and the West Indies. Aaron Lopez and his father-in-law, Jacob

Rodriguez Rivera, excelled in the manufacture and trade of spermaceti candles. Rivera had a secret recipe to make the candles last longer, burn brighter and emit less smoke than their competition. Lopez was considered a master marketer and soon both men were making a small fortune. But Aaron Lopez was also making a fortune off another kind of trading venture. Newport was the foremost colonial port when it came to the African trade. Lopez, like many other merchants who were eager to make as much profit as possible, ventured into this field. Lopez's ships were directly involved in the malevolent Triangle Trade. Lopez also owned interests in distilleries in Newport to manufacture rum, the currency necessary to secure the human cargo on the west coast of Africa. As evil as the enslavement of other humans may have been, Newport merchants, including Aaron Lopez, were making a sizable fortune.

By 1772, Lopez was considered to be the wealthiest businessman in Newport. This is confirmed by the tax roll of that time. He was assessed at the highest rate amongst all the townspeople and fellow merchants. He also owned slaves. By this time there was growing tension between the colonies and England. The winds of revolution had started to blow and Newport would find itself right in the middle of the conflict. Many Newporters were against an armed conflict. They had protection from the crown and were living in a vibrant and wealthy city. These people felt they had a good situation here in Newport, so why make waves? Other prominent citizens did not like the tariffs they were paying on their trading activities. These folks wanted to be independent from England.

War was inevitable and after the British lost control of nearby Boston, they landed a large garrison of roughly two thousand men here in Newport at the end of 1776. Newport's golden age of commerce was over. Many wealthy merchants, especially those who favored independence from the British, fled Newport at this time. Aaron Lopez gathered his family and left for nearby Leicester, Massachusetts. His business activity had ceased after British occupation. They seized his sailing vessels for the war effort and one hundred soldiers bunked in his colonial mansion on Thames Street.

Lopez's fortune took a huge hit. During his exile, he ran a small trading business and general store in Leicester, Massachusetts. Lopez also supplied some of the American troops with necessities during the war for independence. The British who camped in Newport for almost three years were not kind to the city. During the extremely cold winters, they first deforested the island and then tore down some houses for firewood. This occupying force tore down and burned over one hundred colonial structures during their stay. Horses were even stabled in the Old Colony House, the original state capitol building of Rhode Island. Rumors of a large French fleet, now allies with the fledgling American army, forced the British to withdraw their troops at the end of 1779. The French did arrive and camped in the nearly deserted city for a few months before these six thousand troops joined with their American counterparts to force a British surrender at Yorktown, Virginia, in 1781.

With the Revolution over, many exiled former Newporters would return and attempt to reclaim their empires. Aaron Lopez was no exception. He loaded up his family in their carriage and headed for Newport, but karma would finally catch up with him and he would never make it to the site of his former empire. While watering his horse at a place called Scott's Pond in Smithfield, Rhode Island, the animal became spooked and bolted into the center of the pond. Lopez could not swim and drowned on May 27, 1782. Newport's merchant prince was dead. Was he the victim of an accidental drowning or was karma paying him back for profiting from the sale of other human beings into slavery?

AMERICA'S RICHEST FAMILY

The Commodore

Is it possible to turn an initial $100 investment into an empire that is eventually worth over $200 million? This sounds like a bad infomercial on late night TV. It actually did happen and the man who pulled it off was named Cornelius Vanderbilt.

Vanderbilt rose from humble beginnings at the northern tip of Staten Island, New York, directly across a tumultuous channel from the southern tip of Manhattan. As much as Vanderbilt succeeded in becoming a wealthy business titan, he failed miserably as a father, husband and philanthropist.

Cornelius Vanderbilt was born the fourth of nine children to parents Cornelius and Phebe on May 27, 1794. The first Vanderbilts emigrated from Holland to New Amsterdam (renamed New York in 1664) in the late 1630s because of economic turmoil. His unmotivated father ran a small ferry service using a periauger, a small flat-bottom boat that can be rowed or sailed, to shuttle passengers, produce and other goods between Staten Island and lower Manhattan. The elder Vanderbilt seemed happy to make just enough money to get by. This was certainly one trait he did not pass on to his son. His mother, fairly well educated for her time, was always her son Cornelius's closest advisor and the only person he would take advice from. By age eleven, the younger Vanderbilt was running the boat himself, ferrying cargo and passengers to lower Manhattan, as well as learning the tricky tides and currents around New York Harbor. He would also sit on the lawn of his Staten Island home, watching the hundreds of sailing ships pass by as they made their way to and from the busy port area of southern New York City. It is ironic that one day, Vanderbilt himself would control much of the commerce that flowed from the busiest port in the world. Cornelius's road to super wealth began at the age of sixteen, when he was paid $100 to

The Commodore, Cornelius Vanderbilt. This ruthless tycoon was able to turn a $100 investment into a family fortune worth well over $200 million at its peak.

clear a rocky one-acre parcel of the family's property for farming. With this $100 initial investment, he purchased his own boat, and his business career was launched. He had already dropped out of school, instead pursuing local ferry business and operating seven days a week. Cornelius was already showing, even at this young age, his knack for business. During the War of 1812, the young Vanderbilt even received a government contract to ferry soldiers to various forts guarding the harbor area. By this time, he had upgraded to larger schooners, which required even more sailing skill. He was so adept at running his ferryboat in and around the harbor area that he was given the nickname "the Commodore."

He was also gaining a reputation for driving a hard bargain and was developing his business skills around the rough-and-tumble docks of southern Manhattan. This was also the place where Cornelius acquired a taste for ladies of the evening and hard drinking. These two traits would remain with him his entire life.

In 1813, the Commodore's home life was changing as well. On December 13, 1813, Cornelius married his Staten Island neighbor

Sophia Johnson. Sophia also happened to be his first cousin. She would eventually bear him thirteen children, twelve of whom survived until adulthood. Cornelius constantly complained about the lack of male heirs. Only three of his children were boys and he almost constantly complained about their stupidity.

By 1819, steamships were becoming the vessels of choice to ferry passengers around Manhattan, slowly replacing sailing vessels, which were obviously dependant on winds and tides. Steamships could overcome these two hurdles. There was only one problem: the New York legislature granted a thirty-year contract to the steamship inventor Robert Fulton to operate steamships on the busy Hudson River. This monopoly dispute was eventually overturned by the U.S. Supreme Court; by 1829, the Commodore was running his own steamship line on the Hudson River, serving Albany. By 1840, Vanderbilt had over one hundred steamships running goods and passengers along the East Coast and was reportedly the country's largest employer. During the 1849 California Gold Rush, Vanderbilt offered a shorter route to the gold fields via steamship to Nicaragua followed by stagecoach service across the Isthmus and then a steamship again to San Francisco. This route saved over six hundred miles and was half the price of his closest competition. The Commodore always had a knack for seeing a new way of doing things and always undersold his competitors, if necessary, as a way to force them out of business.

By the early 1860s, Cornelius Vanderbilt was already well-to-do. At a time when most men of his wealth and age would retire, the Commodore demonstrated his acumen for investing in up-and-coming new technology. He divested his interest in his steamship line that had already made him a multimillionaire and made a huge bet on a growing transportation option: railroads. This was a time when America was expanding westward and once again Vanderbilt's timing was impeccable. He acquired the New York and Harlem lines as well as the Hudson River and New York Central Railroads. These lines were eventually merged to form the New York Central and Hudson River Railroad in 1869. The Commodore owned the only railroad in and out of America's busiest city. Vanderbilt also built one of the grandest train depots ever seen, the Grand Central Terminal on East Forty-second Street in Midtown Manhattan.

By 1873, the New York Central stretched all the way to Chicago and St. Louis with 740 total track miles, 408 locomotives and 445 passenger cars transporting over 7 million passengers annually. There were also over 9,000 freight cars transporting raw materials, fresh produce and manufactured goods from the nation's heartland to the large East Coast cities, especially New York. The Commodore had a virtual moneymaking empire that was

The Vanderbilt's family fortune was a result of their ownership of the New York Central Railroad. This was the original Grand Central Station on Forty-second Street and Park Avenue. It was demolished around 1900 to make way for the new Grand Central Terminal, which still stands today.

unrivaled on earth. The railroad had total revenue of over $28 million in 1877, while paying their mechanics $1.20 a day while trackmen earned a paltry $0.80 per day.

While the railroad business was booming, the Commodore had some serious setbacks in his personal life. The apple of his eye was his youngest child, George Washington Vanderbilt. Finally, he had a son he could be proud to call his own. He was tall, muscular and handsome, just like the Commodore in his younger days. He was one of the strongest cadets to ever attend West Point and just after his twenty-second birthday, George was commissioned a lieutenant in the Union army. At the Battle of Shiloh, in Tennessee, the strapping young Vanderbilt and eventual heir to the railroad fortune contracted tuberculosis and died on January 1, 1864. Cornelius was devastated. Who would carry on his legacy? His other two sons were useless and the Commodore constantly belittled them. His oldest son William, whom he called "Billy the Blatherskite," was not considered a good businessman and did not have the good looks of his younger brother. He was actually rather short and portly with large mutton chop whiskers. The Commodore's other remaining son was a real headache and constantly gave him trouble. Born Cornelius Jeremiah, "Corneel," as the Commodore called him, was an embarrassment. At eighteen, Corneel started having epileptic seizures, something the Commodore thought showed weakness, which was defiantly beneath a Vanderbilt. The Commodore confided to friends that he thought he was being punished for marrying his cousin. Corneel also developed a gambling addiction, which he would struggle with his entire life. He had a habit of securing loans from the Commodore's friends and gambling with the proceeds. But his father refused to repay the loans, saying they would have to collect from Corneel after he received his inheritance. Corneel eventually ran up so many debts, he had to declare bankruptcy.

In 1868, the Commodore seemed to suffer another family tragedy: his wife Sophia died of a stroke at age seventy-three. But the Commodore may not have been as devastated as one might think. He had been keeping the company of a couple of young women. Victoria Woodhull, who claimed to be a psychic and clairvoyant, said she could communicate with the aging Vanderbilt's long dead mother. The Commodore, who was always looking for an advantage over his business rivals, sought out the advice of the attractive thirty-year-old fortune-teller, especially when trying to predict the direction of volatile railroad stocks. Victoria's twenty-two-year-old sister, Tennessee Claflin, portrayed herself as a magnetic healer, offering to work on the Commodore's old, tired body. She also used other skills she acquired in her previous profession, a high-priced call girl. Tennessee was spending a lot of time with the seventy-three-year-old tycoon, often accompanying him to his railroad office, where she would sit on his lap and pull on his whiskers. Soon enough, the two shyster sisters had the old man's confidence and checkbook. He backed them as stockbrokers and they became the first female firm on Wall Street.

The Commodore would marry again, but not to one of the "Beautiful Brokers of Wall Street" as many had speculated. For his second wife, he chose another cousin, Frankie Crawford of Mobile, Alabama. She had moved to New York City to rebuild her life after the Civil War and decided to look up her cousin Cornelius to help her land on her feet. The seventy-five-year-old grandfather was smitten with his long lost thirty-one-year-old relative and, in 1869, the pair were married in Ontario, Canada, to avoid a media circus in New York. His new wife was deeply religious. She did not approve of the Commodore's card playing, heavy drinking and dalliances into the spiritual world with attractive spiritualists. The old man's days of philandering with the Lady Brokers were over. The richest man in America spent his last few years quietly, often relaxing by driving his prize team of horses around Manhattan and Harlem. By late 1876, the Commodore's health was declining. There were often rumors of his passing, causing railroad stocks to rise and fall with each false report. But the old man was living on borrowed time. His life of heavy drinking and cigar smoking finally caught up with him. On the morning of January 4, 1877, his family was called to his bedside to say their goodbyes. The Commodore was in pain and knew the end was near. He prayed with his wife Frankie, and then called son Billy to his bedside to give him some words of wisdom. Always thinking about business, his last words were, "Keep the money together, keep the central our road. That's my son Bill." With these words of wisdom, and a foreshadowing of the will, the architect of the vast railroad fortune was dead at age eighty-three. An autopsy showed the Commodore's liver and spleen were withered, he had kidney disease and his intestines were inflamed and full of ulcers. It was also revealed after his death that his personal physician had been treating him for syphilis, which may have explained his fits of anger and dementia he experienced later in life. The old man's early habits acquired on the New York waterfront—heavy drinking and socializing with ladies of the evening—finally took their toll. The Commodore was buried in a large family mausoleum on Staten Island, not far from his birthplace. There was one little matter left for the family to take care of: the distribution of the largest estate in history.

After the funeral, the family returned to a relative's parlor and the Commodore's personal lawyer, Charles Rapallo, read the will aloud. To Frankie, his young wife, he left a paltry $500,000 plus the modest Manhattan home. Each of his nine daughters received some railroad bonds and trust funds of a few thousand dollars. Crazy Corneel received only the income from a $200,000 trust fund to support himself. He later sued the estate and was paid an additional $500,000 in New York Central bonds. To celebrate his newfound money, Corneel took a trip around the world and then went to Hartford to oversee work on his new house. He spent the night of April 1, 1882, gambling heavily and apparently losing heavily as well. How much did he lose? Enough to return to his hotel room and commit suicide by shooting himself. A few other family friends and loyal employees were bequeathed small amounts of money as well. Before his death, the Commodore left $50,000 to a nondenominational church in lower Manhattan and $1 million to Central University of Nashville, which quickly renamed itself Vanderbilt University in honor of its benefactor. The last clause of the will bequeathed the remainder of the estate, roughly $95 million, to William H. Vanderbilt. The son the Commodore called "Billy the Blatherskite" and a stupid blockhead had overnight become the richest man in the world.

William Henry

At fifty-six years of age, William Henry Vanderbilt inherited $95 million and was running the New York Central Railroad. The Commodore had counseled his son right before his death, "Any fool can make a fortune, it takes a man of brains to hold on to it after he's made it." Just a few years earlier, the overbearing father had thought his son Billy was useless. The Commodore exiled Billy to Staten Island to run a small railroad that was unprofitable. Much to the Commodore's surprise, Billy had cut costs and increased ridership in the fledgling line enough to be profitable and increase the stock price. The Commodore was impressed and thought he had misjudged his oldest son. He was impressed enough to leave him the bulk of the vast fortune. Critics were sure that bumbling Billy would ride the Central into bankruptcy. There was labor strife early in his tenure as chairman of the railroad. Conductors and brakemen had threatened to strike. But Billy knew his employees were loyal and quickly offered $100,000 to be divided amongst his devoted help. The bonus worked and a strike was averted for a measly hundred grand. This is something the Commodore would have never done; he preferred to fight rather than compromise. Billy was proving he was no idiot.

During the 1880s, the New York Central was facing increased competition from upstart railroads. Using a tactic his father employed, William Henry started his own price wars, trying to put the competition out of business by cutting prices. He also did one thing his father would never do: he cut the dividend of New York Central's stock, causing a near panic on Wall Street. He also suffered a huge public relations blunder when a reporter asked William if he was considering ending a fast-moving mail train from New York to Chicago to save money. The line was unprofitable and the reporter kept pressing him whether he was working for the public or the stockholder. An incensed William Henry finally shot back, "The public be damned. I am working for my stockholders. If the public wants the train so bad, why don't they support it?" The damage was done. He was trying to express a business philosophy but all anyone focused on was the quote, "The Public Be Damned!" The gap between the common man and the wealthy tycoon was never larger.

Business on the railroad was booming and the conservative William accounted for every penny. He lived rather frugally for a man of his vast wealth and in six years had nearly doubled his inheritance to almost $200 million. He had made in six short years what it took his father a lifetime to accumulate. William Henry controlled more money than the entire U.S.

William Henry Vanderbilt was the principal heir of the Commodore's massive fortune. He was able to double his $95 million inheritance to well over $200 million in only eight short years. Unfortunately, he died in 1885, just eight years after his father, at the age of sixty-four.

Treasury. The long hours of running the line, as well as increased competition and public relations battles, had taken their tolls on his health. William was a man in his early sixties, yet confided to friends he felt like an eighty-year-old. In 1883, William retired and turned over control of the New York Central to his two oldest sons, Cornelius II and William K. Vanderbilt. He continued collecting art and supporting various charitable causes, including founding the Metropolitan Opera in New York City and enlarging Vanderbilt University. Apparently, the strain of running the family business had already taken its toll. Unfortunately, William did not get to enjoy his fortune very long; he suffered a stroke and died December 8, 1885, only eight short years after his father. Once again the Vanderbilt fortune was about to be divided.

Cornelius II

If the first two wealthy Vanderbilt generations were the builders of the family fortune, the next two generations could certainly be considered the free spenders. The heirs to the railroad fortune would go on a mansion-building spree unparalleled in American history. Cornelius II and his wife, Alice, built a 140-room mansion on New York City's Fifth Avenue, now the site of the Bergdorf Goodman department store.

Not to be outdone by sister-in-law Alva and her newly built Marble House on Newport's famed Bellevue Avenue, Cornelius commissioned family architect Richard Morris Hunt to build a summer cottage even more spectacular. Money was no object; Cornelius II had received nearly $70 million from his father's estate. The result was the magnificent Breakers mansion, built on the site of a smaller wooden structure that had burned in 1892. Wife Alice was demanding of architect Hunt. Everything had to be done to her high standards and in record time, and it must be bigger than sister-in-law Alva's Marble House. Construction began in the spring of 1893, with over two thousand laborers and artisans working around the clock to reach Alice's completion date of the summer of 1895. The property was so elaborate that entire rooms were built in France, shipped to Newport and reassembled inside the Breakers. The property was so large it took up one acre of land and would contain seventy rooms. The mansion would make its scheduled opening date, August 14, 1895, for the debutante ball of daughter Gertrude. The Breakers's opening may have been the downfall

William Henry's two oldest sons split the bulk of the Vanderbilt fortune. His oldest son, Cornelius II, built a gigantic mansion at 1 West Fifty-seventh Street and Fifth Avenue in Manhattan. It is now the site of the Bergdorf Goodman department store.

of family architect Richard Morris Hunt. He died two weeks before the Breakers's completion date. Hunt was the Vanderbilts' architect of choice, building their Fifth Avenue mansions as well as the Breakers and the Marble House in Newport. He was also responsible for George Vanderbilt's monster estate, the Biltmore, near Asheville, North Carolina.

Cornelius II would only get to enjoy his magnificent summer palace the year it opened. In 1896, the workaholic chairman of the New York Central would suffer a debilitating stroke, be confined to a wheelchair and be dead from a cerebral hemorrhage by 1899. He was only fifty-five years of age. The Vanderbilt fortune, which seemed like a blessing, was turning into a curse. Wife Alice was not able to afford her gigantic Fifth Avenue mansion on the income of her $7 million trust fund. The expenses and taxes were too much for her to pay. Multiple attempts to sell the mansion failed and it was torn down in 1925, to make way for the commercial district spreading up Fifth Avenue. Alice moved to a modest townhouse farther up the Avenue. She constantly wore black to mourn her husband's death, rarely opened the Breakers in the summer and was seldom seen in public. She died in 1934.

Cornelius Vanderbilt II had so much money that he built this massive summer home, the Breakers, which was only used for six weeks during the summer season. The home is now a museum and is Rhode Island's most visited tourist attraction. *Photo courtesy of the author.*

Cornelius II and Alice's children also suffered some bizarre misfortunes. Their oldest son William died of typhoid fever in 1892, while attending Yale University. He was only twenty-one. Their second son, Cornelius III, was disinherited for marrying a woman named Grace Wilson. The parents did not approve of Grace because she was six years older than "Neily" and was considered much too worldly. There was also speculation that Grace Wilson's father may have had a bad reputation as a Civil War profiteer. Their third son Alfred, the heir to the bulk of his father's fortune, went down on the *Lusitania* (see chapter 13). Then there was their fourth son Reginald, the black sheep of the Vanderbilt family.

Reginald

If there was ever one person who epitomized the lazy and spoiled rich kid, it was Reginald Claypoole Vanderbilt, born in 1880, with a platinum spoon in his mouth. Reggie (to his friends) learned quickly at Yale he could become popular by racing horses, spending thousands of dollars on drinking sprees and ladies of the evening and gambling on sporting events. At twenty-one, he inherited $7.5 million from his father's estate. By the end of that evening, he had lost $70,000 at Richard Canfield's illegal gambling hall in New York City. This was just the start of the losses. Years later, when police raided the gambling establishment, they found $400,000 of IOUs from Reggie. He never worked a day in his life. When asked his occupation, he would reply, "Gentleman." By age twenty-three, he was diagnosed with cirrhosis of the liver, no doubt from his fondness for brandy milk punch. Reggie's real passion was in raising show horses and polo ponies. He bought a 280-acre horse farm outside of Newport. He also built a racetrack on the property to train his prized animals. Reggie had no responsibility and his main focus was to keep from being bored. He was also notorious for speeding around the Newport area and local farmers would throw rocks at his car to attempt to slow him down. In New York City, he had hit at least five pedestrians, killing two. Because he was a Vanderbilt, he was never prosecuted. Reggie also abandoned his first wife and daughter in Paris in 1912, sailing back to New York without even a note to explain his departure or money for their return. He was truly a despicable person. But no matter what he did, his mother Alice always looked the other way or bailed him out with money. Reggie was still the baby and could do no wrong. In 1922, Reggie was forty-two and New York and Newport's most eligible bachelor. Despite all his shortcomings, he was still a Vanderbilt.

In January 1922, Reggie would fall in love with seventeen-year-old Gloria Morgan. When Reggie wanted something, he usually got it. This time he

The wild child of the Vanderbilt family, Reggie, and his nemesis, the automobile. He would constantly speed, drive drunk and often strike pedestrians. Because he was a Vanderbilt, he was never prosecuted for his indiscretions.

wanted to marry the beautiful Miss Morgan. The naïve seventeen-year-old gladly accepted, even though Reggie explained he had squandered all his inheritance. His $5 million trust fund was to support his daughter from his first marriage. The only way Gloria would be supported was to have a child with Reggie; then she could also have access to the income from his airtight trust fund. Reggie also explained to his young wife-to-be that having a child with him would be difficult; he was not a well man from his excessive lifestyle. But Gloria did not care. She loved Reggie. She gave birth to a daughter, little Gloria, on February 20, 1924. The newlyweds' bliss would be short-lived. On a trip to Europe the next spring, Reggie experienced serious nosebleeds. After seeing a doctor, the diagnosis was serious: his liver was severely damaged. The doctor's prognosis was no more alcohol, period. Gloria tried to keep Reggie in Europe as long as possible and away from his drinking buddies. Reggie would not hear of it; he would be back in Newport by August for the annual horse show. In September 1925, Gloria headed to Chile to visit her ailing grandmother. Reggie was on his own and could not control himself. He made his rounds, including drinks at the exclusive Newport Reading Room. He then headed back to his estate, Sandy Point

Farm. Gloria called to check on him before she boarded her ship to Chile and a strange voice answered the phone. It was Reggie's nurse. Gloria knew something was awry and immediately returned to Rhode Island. When she arrived at 5:00 a.m., her mother-in-law Alice's Rolls-Royce was in the driveway and she expected the worse. She rushed inside but was too late; Reggie was dead. The hemorrhaging that killed him was so violent his esophagus exploded, splattering blood all over his bedroom. Young Gloria had lost her husband and Alice Vanderbilt had lost her favorite son.

There is one thing young Gloria gained from Reggie's death: she was now entitled to the income from his trust fund that was to be used for daughter Gloria's expenses. But the money went to everything but little Gloria. Mama Gloria used her monthly allowances to live a life of extravagance. She traveled to Paris, Monte Carlo, London, New York and Hollywood, and partied at just about every nightclub in these cities. Soon an insolvent German prince was also traveling around with Gloria, living off her child's trust fund. Another woman, a nurse named Keislich, also traveled with the family, to take care of young Gloria.

Many influential people were taking notice of Gloria's partying ways. One such interested observer was Reggie's sister, Gertrude. She knew Gloria was only keeping little Gloria around to live off her trust fund. The wild Gloria cared little about the child's well-being. Gertrude eventually sued for custody of her dead brother's little girl. She was certainly well funded to raise a child. Gertrude was married to part-time Newport resident Harry Paine Whitney, heir to the Standard Oil fortune. She was also an art lover, eventually opening the Whitney Museum of Modern Art in New York City. But at this moment, her attention was focused on her little niece.

The custody trial began in a packed New York Supreme Court building on October 1, 1934. Nurse Keislich was called to testify and reported that the family lived in a rat-infested apartment while in Paris. The nurse also reported Gloria was always bringing nightclub people home after the bars closed and slept until well into the afternoon. A maid also testified that she once brought breakfast to Gloria and found her in bed with another woman who was kissing her like a lover. The courtroom gasped in amazement. Reporters ran out of the courtroom to call in the shocking headlines. The judge even interviewed ten-year-old Gloria to find out her feelings. She revealed she loved living at Aunt Gertrude's country estate on Long Island and had no desire to return to the custody of her partying mother. The judge had little choice. Aunt Gertrude was awarded custody and Gloria Morgan Claypoole Vanderbilt lost the income from little Gloria's trust fund. She would eventually move to Hollywood and die virtually penniless in 1965. Mother and daughter would never reconcile. Little Gloria's claim to fame was eventually starting a design company, which produced tightfitting Vanderbilt jeans in the early 1980s. Her fourth marriage, to Wyatt Cooper, produced a son, Anderson Cooper, of CNN fame.

The Vanderbilt Legacy

There is very little left today from a fortune that had once reached $200 million. It is almost unfathomable that a fortune worth over $150 billion in today's inflation-adjusted world would no longer exist. The Vanderbilt wealth was $100 billion greater than today's richest American, Bill Gates. How could so much money just disappear? One of the major reasons the money did not last was the passing of the Sixteenth Amendment in 1913: "The Congress shall have power to lay and collect taxes on incomes, from whatever source derived, without apportionment among the several States, and without regard to any census or enumeration." Essentially, Congress had passed an income tax, something previous generations did not have to contend with. (Ironically, Rhode Island was one of the states that never ratified this amendment.) Inheritance taxes also took away huge chunks of family wealth when it passed between generations. The biggest factor in the decline of the Vanderbilt family fortune was its strong ties to the New York Central Railroad. Most of the trust funds were funded with the railroad's stock, which was high during the peak years of railroad traffic. The stock also paid a steady 8 percent dividend that helped to fund the lavish lifestyles.

But railroads, especially in the early twentieth century, were losing their appeal. Cars were becoming more affordable and the general public preferred their own cars to riding the rails. Later in the twentieth century, air travel would essentially end the train's role as a long-distance carrier. The New York Central's stock price hit a high of $258 per share on September 3, 1929. Two weeks after the October stock market crash, the stock was at $160. By 1941, the stock was at $25 per share. The family had tied too much of their wealth to one company's stock, especially one that was past its prime with outmoded technology. The once proud and profitable New York Central was merged with a rival railroad in 1968. The newly formed line, the Penn Central, could not stem the tide of declining revenues, amassing over $100 million in losses in its first year of operation. By 1970, the company declared bankruptcy and all rail lines and assets were reorganized into the government's Consolidated Rail Corporation, Conrail. No one in these subsequent generations was savvy enough or had the foresight to invest in some new company or technology that would have carried the Vanderbilt wealth well into the future, like the Commodore had done roughly seventy

These gates are the only remains of Reggie's horse farm in nearby Portsmouth, Rhode Island. Sandy Point Farm was the location where Reggie perished; essentially, his esophagus exploded from a hemorrhage resulting from alcohol abuse. *Photo courtesy of the author.*

years earlier. The Vanderbilts of this era thought the money would last forever and built monuments to a fortune they had not earned themselves. They squandered their money on building mansions or lived for the moment, like Reggie, without much consideration of the family's legacy.

Some of these monuments to excess still stand. The Preservation Society of Newport County now owns two former Vanderbilt mansions and they are open to the public for tours. If you visit Newport, be sure to visit the Breakers or the Marble House to see for yourself what America's one-time richest family had created and then squandered. The Breakers was sold to the Preservation Society in 1972, for a modest $365,000 (it cost over $7 million to construct), with the stipulation that Vanderbilt descendants would have use of a third-floor apartment during the summer season. The heirs still use it to this day. The Breakers remains the largest tourist attraction in Rhode Island. As you tour these grand properties, remember the Commodore's prophetic words: "Any fool can make a fortune; it takes a man of brains to hold onto it after he's made it."

THE QUEEN OF
THE QUEEN OF RESORTS

Because Newport, Rhode Island, had become the preeminent summer resort for America's super wealthy and influential citizens of the late nineteenth century, it earned the nickname "the Queen of Resorts." And there was one woman who ruled over the social scenes of both New York City and Newport like royalty. Her name was Mrs. Astor. Caroline Schermerhorn was born in New York City, in 1830, to a well-established and wealthy family. Her uncle owned the shipping docks of the busy South Street Seaport area in lower Manhattan. Caroline also married well, tying the knot with William Backhouse Astor Jr. in 1854. Mr. Astor's grandfather, John Jacob, was a penniless immigrant when he arrived in America in 1784. He parlayed a fur-trading empire into vast tracts of New York City real estate, becoming one of the richest men in America. (The Astors were also known as the slumlords of Manhattan, owning numerous tenements full of newly arrived immigrants.) Mrs. Astor now had the money and cachet to head New York and Newport's social scenes.

In 1862, she built a large and fashionable brownstone mansion at 350 Fifth Avenue with a grand ballroom ready to entertain New York's elite families. (The site of this mansion is now the Empire State Building.)

Along with her social minister, Ward McAllister, Mrs. Astor decided who and what was fashionable and could be included in their exclusive club of upper-class families, the "Four Hundred." This was the number of New Yorkers they deemed fashionable enough to rub elbows with Mrs. Astor and with each other. Coincidently, it was also the number of people who could fit in the ballroom. Mrs. Astor only liked to socialize with "old money" and did not care for these upstart railroad millionaires, like the Vanderbilts. To be a member of the "Four Hundred," a family must be able trace its wealth and lineage at least three generations without being tainted by any work. Mrs. Astor felt the money needed to "cool off" properly before one's inclusion.

Mrs. Astor was the reigning Queen of New York and Newport high society until a stroke and dementia ended her rule in 1908.

Mrs. Astor, by all outward appearances, would not be the kind of person who throngs of people would beg to be around. She was considered by her peers to be a little chubby and a little short, with a jutting jaw and a big nose. Physical appearances aside, Mrs. Astor made wearing jewelry an art form, although it was not proper during the day. Jewelry was reserved for the evening and she took it to an outrageous level. Mrs. Astor was known for wearing a diamond tiara and a triple-stranded diamond necklace as well as a diamond-encrusted stomacher, which once belonged to Marie Antoinette, stretched around her midsection. Mrs. Astor would also never be seen in public without her black wig, covering her graying hair. Some partygoers thought she was so overloaded with jewelry that she had difficulty walking. The annual ball held in Mrs. Astor's New York City ballroom was the apex of each social season. An invitation to this event cemented one's status in the elite "Four Hundred." If a person was snubbed for the ball, chances were his high-society days were over. After dinner, Mrs. Astor would hold court on her long couch—affectionately called "the throne"—and greet visitors, paying special attention to guests she deemed worthy of her time.

In 1881, Mrs. Astor turned her attention to Newport. With her husband's money, she purchased an oceanfront cottage, called Beechwood, on prestigious Bellevue Avenue, for the paltry sum of $180,000. She then hired famed architect Richard Morris Hunt to enlarge the ballroom to facilitate summer parties for the "Four Hundred." The price tag for the ballroom was $2 million. But, after all, it was Mr. Astor's money and he was not interested in the frivolity of these lavish parties. As long as Mrs. Astor kept busy with her social events, Mr. Astor was free to entertain young ladies on his yacht, the *Nourmahal*.

Of course, the highlight of the summer season in Newport was Mrs. Astor's summer ball. The fortunate invitees were entertained by large orchestras, ten-course meals eaten off of gold plates and waited on by blue-liveried footmen copied from England's Windsor Castle. Nothing was too good for the Queen of High Society. Mrs. Astor and her trusted social advisor, Ward McAllister, would dominate the party and social scene through the mid-1890s. McAllister was the authority of his era when it came to social etiquette and commented on everything from the proper way to serve champagne to the necessity of hiring a French chef. McAllister—with his "Mystic Rose," Mrs. Astor—had transformed the simple seaside resort of Newport, Rhode Island, into a mecca for the pleasure-seeking, status-conscious rich of the Gilded Age. McAllister even earned the nickname "Ward Make-a-Lister" because of his obsession with the "Four Hundred."

Perhaps McAllister was a little too pompous when he wrote a book called *Society as I Have Found It*, wherein he revealed many of high society's secrets and eccentricities. The book outraged many of the movers and shakers of the era and McAllister was ostracized from the Old Guard. He died of a heart attack while dining alone at New York's Union Club in 1895. The next day was a grand Astor ball, but the Queen would never even consider cancelling. In the immortal words of McAllister himself, "A dinner invitation once accepted is a sacred obligation. If you die before the dinner takes place, your executor must attend."

Mrs. Astor went on entertaining until 1905, when she threw her last great ball. She had a serious fall down a flight of marble stairs after suffering a stroke and withdrew permanently from society. Suffering from dementia, Mrs. Astor wandered the halls of her Fifth Avenue mansion, still diamond-encrusted and calling out to partygoers and long dead guests who were no longer there. Perhaps she was reliving her glory days as the reigning Queeen of High Society. Mrs. Astor passed away in 1908, at the age of seventy-eight, and was buried in New York's prestigious Trinity Church cemetery. Even in death, Mrs. Astor had to stand out. Her thirty-nine-foot tombstone dominated the small church burying ground. Her son, John Jacob Astor IV, would carry forward the Astor crown but his reign would be short-lived. Mr. Astor and his new bride booked a passage on a new luxury liner, the *Titanic* (see chapter 12).

Mrs. Astor's days of entertaining were over but she left her mark on the Queen of Resorts. The reputation Newport has today as one of the finest resort cities on the East Coast can be traced to Mrs. Astor, and her "Four Hundred," who put it on the map as the place where the world's elite summered. And with Mrs. Astor's death, other socialites rushed in to fill the void as reigning Queen of Newport society, with the parties becoming even more elaborate and bizarre than even the Queen herself could have imagined.

WICKED ALVA

Alva Erskine Smith was born in Mobile, Alabama, on January 17, 1853, to a fairly well-to-do Southern family. Alva's father was a wealthy cotton broker who moved his family to Paris to avoid the atrocities of the Civil War and the destruction of the Southern economy that would follow. Alva was educated at French finishing schools, where she learned proper etiquette and witnessed firsthand the pomp and circumstance at the royal palaces throughout France. This extravagant style of entertaining would serve her well later in life.

The family returned to the United States in 1869, when Alva was sixteen, choosing New York City as their home. The family still owned slaves from their pre–Civil War days in Mobile. This may have influenced young Alva's relationships with people she felt were inferior to her. Having total control over someone at such a young age may have contributed to her obsession with power and control. Alva always had to have her own way; if she did not, she would throw violent tantrums. She was even known to chase after boys who had teased her excessively, to give them a physical beating.

In the summer of 1874, Alva took a trip that would change her life forever. She traveled to White Sulfur Springs, West Virginia, a popular resort area where wealthy bachelors would often vacation. This was also the spot where Southern belles would look for rich husbands. Alva landed a big one, becoming engaged to William Kissam Vanderbilt, heir to the railroad fortune. Their wedding was held on April 20, 1875, and was one of the grandest and most expensive weddings New York society had witnessed. Alva always told close friends, "First marry for money then marry for love." Alva struck gold with first husband Willie K. Vanderbilt. His grandfather was the richest man in the world. The Commodore's fortune was estimated at $100 million. Alva went on a mansion-building spree to show the world the Vanderbilts had arrived. A grand mansion on Fifth

Alva Vanderbilt Belmont was a pugnacious social climber who usually got what she wanted. Before her death, she requested that all of her photos as a society diva be burned. She wanted to be remembered as an activist for women's suffrage.

Avenue was soon constructed by Richard Morris Hunt as well as a large country estate on Long Island. The one thing Alva coveted was inclusion in the elite "Four Hundred," controlled by society diva Mrs. Astor. The Vanderbilt nouveau riche wealth was not qualified for inclusion; the family was involved in railroads, a trade that was a no-no in Mrs. Astor's world. Alva usually got her own way, and hatched an elaborate plan to make Mrs. Astor come begging. To show off her new grand mansion, Alva planned a grand costume ball and invited twelve hundred of New York's finest citizens, except Mrs. Astor. Mrs. Astor's daughter Carrie had been practicing a dance routine called a quadrille for her debutante debut but could not be invited because her mother had not formally accepted the Vanderbilts into society. Finally, Mrs. Astor called on Alva and was granted a formal invitation. The party was held on March 26, 1883, with all guests arriving in elaborate costumes. Ironically, Alva and Mrs. Astor both chose to dress as Venetian noblewomen. Sister-in-law Alice Vanderbilt dressed as the Statue of Liberty, complete with battery-powered lights. Only two guests were not required to wear a costume—family patriarch William Henry Vanderbilt and former President Ulysses S. Grant.

New York newspapers hailed the costume ball as the greatest the city had ever seen and may have cost upward of $250,000. This was a small price for Alva to pay for inclusion in New York's high society. And she was just beginning; Alva had her sights set on much loftier goals.

In 1885, Alva's father-in-law, William Henry Vanderbilt, died unexpectedly and left an amount of money to his heirs that was almost unimaginable. His second son and Alva's husband, Willie K., received a staggering $55 million. She now had the bankroll to match her ambitious dreams. In 1888, the Vanderbilts started construction of a summer home in Newport that was emblematic of their wealth and newfound place in high society. Family architect Richard Morris Hunt was chosen for this monumental task and felt energized at undertaking such a large project where money was no object. Hunt chose to model this property after the Petit Trianon, a palace at Versailles. Hundreds of Italian marble workers and artisans were brought to Newport to work on this grand project. They were also sworn to secrecy and high fences were erected around the work site. Alva wanted the property's unveiling to awe even the wealthiest of the Newport elite. A special dock and warehouse were constructed on Newport harbor to accommodate the large shipments of marble arriving from all over the world. Alva was a demanding client, even for the experienced Richard Morris Hunt. He was used to dealing with a wealthy and difficult clientele but Alva was in a league of her own. She had a hand in every aspect of the mansion's construction, down to the minutest detail. Alva did not care; it was her money and she

The usually reserved Alice Vanderbilt of the Breakers lets her hair down a little for Alva Vanderbilt's famous costume ball. Only two people who attended the 1883 festivities did not have to wear costumes: family patriarch William Henry Vanderbilt and former President Ulysses S. Grant.

wanted it done her way! During the mansion's construction, husband Willie also got a new toy. He purchased the largest steam yacht ever built, 285 feet long and 32 feet wide, and named it the *Alva* in honor of his wife. It was so large that on a family cruise to the Mediterranean, the Turkish navy fired upon it, thinking it was an enemy's warship. This was a contentious time in the Vanderbilts' marriage. Alva had heard rumors of Willie's philandering with young ladies on his new yacht, so she decided to keep him occupied and focused on family. Her solution was that the family would take a long cruise together to rekindle their love while waiting for their grand Newport mansion's completion. Besides Willie and Alva, these cruises would include their three children: Consuelo, William K. II and Harold. Often, close family friends would come along as well on their trips to Europe, Turkey and even Egypt. One frequent traveler was Willie's horse racing buddy and fellow millionaire, Oliver Hazard Perry Belmont. The less attention Willie showed Alva, Oliver Belmont seemed to pick up the slack, becoming enamored with his good friend's wife. On a trip from Bar Harbor, Maine, to Newport, the *Alva* was accidentally rammed by another ship and sank off of the south shore of Cape Cod. It was certainly foreshadowing for their relationship. After rescue, Willie's first telegram was to order an even larger yacht, the *Valiant*. His marriage to Alva was sinking, but Willie was rich and handsome and could care less about his wife's needs.

In August of 1892, the Marble House was finally unveiled to Newport's summer crowd and the vote was unanimous: no one had ever seen anything like it. Alva was officially handed the "cottage" as a gift for her thirty-ninth birthday. The mansion featured a two-story Siena marble entry hall, a gold ballroom where even the chandeliers were covered in gold leaf and a dining room with pink Numidian marble walls and bronze-cast dining chairs. The chairs were so heavy that a footman stood behind each one to assist the guests. The total cost of this summer home was an unbelievable $11 million, with $7 million of the budget going to procure marble. A similar property would be almost impossible to build today. Besides the cost, $150 million in today's money, craftsmen and artisans capable of building such a masterpiece would be difficult to obtain.

Alva decided, in one last attempt to save her marriage, that the family would again cruise aboard the new yacht, *Valiant*, to India. Once again, admirer Oliver Belmont was along for the ride. Rumors had been persistent that husband Willie had been openly dating a woman named Nellie Neustretter in Paris. This young French mademoiselle was also a well-known prostitute. Willie had even set Nellie up with an apartment and living allowance. Alva had had enough; the trip was cut short and the couple separated for good. Alva did something most women in her day

Alva's summer cottage, the $11 million Marble House. First husband William K. Vanderbilt gave the mansion to Alva for her thirty-ninth birthday. The couple divorced soon after the mansion's completion and it remained unoccupied for many years. *Photo courtesy of the author.*

would not even imagine: she sued for divorce on the grounds of adultery. It was revealed during divorce proceedings that Willie thought Alva was also unfaithful; he came home early one day and found good friend Oliver Belmont hiding in his bedroom closet. But a divorce was granted and Alva received a $2.5 million settlement and $100,000 in annual income plus the Marble House. Alva was immediately ostracized by the Vanderbilts but was still influential in Newport society.

Perhaps as a diversion from the divorce, Alva turned her attention to her young daughter Consuelo. There was a growing trend among the newly formed millionaires of the Industrial Revolution to marry their children off to European nobility to gain a royal title to legitimize their wealth. Usually, the nobility were rich in title only and actively campaigned to become hitched to an affluent American debutante. Alva, always looking for a way to advance her family socially, was openly accepting offers for her youthful daughter's hand in marriage. There was one problem with Alva's grand plan: Consuelo was already in love with a young man named Winthrop Rutherfurd. Rutherfurd was a practicing lawyer, tall, handsome and possessed an impressive family lineage. He was a descendant of John Winthrop, the first governor of Massachusetts. But Alva would not hear of it; he was not of noble descent and she forbade her daughter from seeing "Winty." When Alva discovered plans that the couple may elope, she literally locked poor Consuelo in her room and guarded her twenty-four hours a day. Consuelo was a prisoner of the Marble House until Alva could handpick a husband with the proper imperial qualifications. Alva had made her choice. She settled on Charles Richard John Spencer-Churchill, the Ninth Duke of Marlborough and first cousin of future British Prime Minister Winston Churchill. But Consuelo wasn't interested. She loved Winthrop. Alva, who always had to have her way, first threatened to murder young Winthrop Rutherfurd. When that threat didn't persuade her daughter, Alva feigned a mortal illness and begged Consuelo to grant her a dying wish. Alva had finally tricked her daughter to concede and the couple was wed on November 6, 1895, at Saint Thomas Church in New York City, in front of hundreds of dignitaries and invited guests, including a miraculously cured Alva. Many of the guests reported that during the ceremony they could hear muffled sobs coming from under the eighteen-year-old Consuelo's veil.

Alva finally got her wish: her daughter married a duke and gained a royal title for the family, legitimizing their newfound wealth. The duke got what he wanted: a $2.5 million dowry to refurbish his massive estate, Blenheim Palace near Oxfordshire. The only loser in the matter was poor Consuelo. She was forced to marry a man she did not love, then move to England to live in a vast, empty castle in a loveless marriage. Consuelo did her duty as the Ninth Duchess of Marlborough, bearing her husband two sons, including his successor to the royal title. But she was miserable and the Duke mistreated her constantly. In a shocking move, she separated from her husband after twelve years of marriage; she had finally had enough abuse. Consuelo was officially divorced, in 1921, so she could finally marry for love. She tied the knot with a French aviator named Jacque Balsan and lived a much happier life outside of Paris. The marriage was eventually annulled in 1926. Alva would later concede that forcing her daughter to marry the duke was one of her biggest regrets.

With Consuelo's wedding behind her, Alva was free to focus on her own nuptials. In 1896, she married banking heir and old family friend Oliver Hazard Perry Belmont, the man she may have been intimate with during her previous marriage. The couple moved into Belmont's Newport mansion Belcourt, right down the street from the Marble House. Marble House would be rarely used over the next decade, except to store Alva's extra clothes and to use the laundry facility, which was superior to Belcourt's. Belmont had been single for many years after a previous divorce and

The beautiful Consuelo Vanderbilt, Alva's only daughter. The wicked Alva forced Consuelo to marry a man she didn't love because he possessed a royal title.

modeled his Newport mansion after a French hunting lodge. Also an avid horseman, he had the first floor of his mansion designed with stables for his prized trotters, with an entryway large enough to drive his carriage right into the first floor of the mansion. (The Belmont Stakes horse race in New York is named in the family's honor.) But Alva was now the woman of the house and a multimillion-dollar renovation was in store for Belcourt, which included a Gothic dining room for entertaining and stables outside of the mansion for the horses.

The Belmonts lived quietly and with little controversy until Oliver's sudden death in 1908. Alva needed a cause to devote her time and energy to, as well as her roughly $10 million inheritance. In 1909, she founded the Political Quality League as a way to campaign for the women's suffrage movement. The shuttered Marble House was even reopened as a meeting place for fundraisers and for the growing crusade pushing for equal voting rights. The culmination of Alva's marching, picketing and fundraising was the ratification of the Nineteenth Amendment to the U.S. Constitution on August 26, 1920: "The right of citizens of the United States to vote shall not be denied or abridged by the United States or by any State on account of sex."

Alva had finally used her tenacity and almost limitless resources to accomplish something for the good of many, instead of for her own materialistic and self-centered whims.

After her crusade, Alva moved to Paris to be close to her daughter. They seemed to have a closer relationship later in life. Alva died of a stroke on January 26, 1933, in Paris and her body was returned to New York for her funeral. The Mass was held at Saint Thomas Church, at the same location where a weeping Consuelo had married the Duke of Marlborough. Alva also had twenty honorary female pallbearers from the National Woman's Party, a group she had funded extensively in the fight for equal voting rights.

With Alva's death, her three children grew closer. Her oldest son, Willie K. II, would continue his life's passion of exploring the world's oceans on his yacht. He was also renowned for a collection of marine species, which are now in a museum at his former estate in Centerport on Long Island. Her youngest son, Harold Stirling, successfully defended the America's Cup three times, invented the game of contact bridge and was the last Vanderbilt to serve on the New York Central's board of directors. Consuelo and husband Jacque returned to the United States with the growing political tension in Europe and settled in South Florida, near Palm Beach.

Just before Alva's death, she sold her Newport mansion, which cost $11 million to construct, for the miniscule amount of $100,000. In 1963, her son Harold reacquired the Marble House, and donated it to the Preservation

Society in memory of his mother. It serves as a reminder that things that seem so important and significant in one stage of a person's life can become vain and worthless later on. Before Alva's death, she requested that all paintings depicting her as a young socialite be burned. She wanted to be remembered as a fighter for equal voting rights. One important lesson we can take from Alva's life is that no matter how poorly you treat your loved ones, even if you think you are doing the right thing, they will forgive your missteps and that there is always time for redemption.

MRS. FISH

If Mrs. Astor's parties were generally considered boring and Alva Vanderbilt's social gatherings were extravagant, then Mrs. Fish's get-togethers were totally bizarre. Mrs. Fish was one of the countless members of frolicsome society who migrated annually from New York to Newport for the summer season. But Mrs. Fish was anything but the typical society maiden. Mamie, as her close friends knew her, had certainly married well. Her husband was Stuyvesant Fish, the president of the Illinois Central Railroad and a direct descendant of old New Yorker Peter Stuyvesant. When Mrs. Fish was asked which railroad her husband was associated with, she replied, "I don't know, one line or the other. They are all the same to me." She did not look the part a leading hostess of the gilded era. She was a little rotund and looked somewhat frumpy in her fashionable merrymaking attire. She also dealt with guests a little more candidly when they arrived at her home. Her popular greeting was, "Howdy Do, Howdy Do, make yourselves at home, and believe me, no one wishes you were there, more than I do." Mrs. Fish was sarcastic, sharp-tongued and detested long, drawn out affairs. She pioneered the fifty-minute dinner party, where guests complained their plates were barely cleared before servants quickly took the dish away. Mrs. Fish's parties were more casual than other high-society members were used to; she encouraged guests to call each other by first names. She disliked the formality that was omnipresent along Newport's Bellevue Avenue. Mrs. Fish wanted folks to relax and enjoy themselves. She was also one of the first hostesses to invite visiting dignitaries, famous actors and noted celebrities to share in the festivities.

With the waning of Mrs. Astor's preeminence as queen of the social scene, Mrs. Fish was one of the new leaders of society in the early 1900s. And with social minister Ward McAllister's death, a new man of the party-planning scene emerged, Harry Lehr. If McAllister was traditional and ceremonial,

Lehr was the opposite. He preferred events to be frivolous and spontaneous. Paired with Mrs. Fish, they formed the dynamic duo of the social scene. Mrs. Fish's Newport headquarters was a mansion on Ocean Drive called Crossways, just above the ultra-exclusive Bailey's Beach.

On one occasion, when Grand Duke Boris visited Newport, Mrs. Fish sent out invitations for a dinner in his honor. Unfortunately, she never checked the duke's social calendar; he was already attending a party given by another socialite. There were two hundred guests at Crossways expecting the presence of a Russian dignitary. Mrs. Fish announced to her visitors that the duke could not attend, but had a replacement: the czar of Russia. Suddenly the doors were flung open and in walked His Imperial Majesty, dressed in regal robes, a crown on his head and carrying a scepter. Guests, including New York Senator Chauncey Depew and J.P. Morgan, began to bow in honor of their guest, and then roared with laughter when they realized they had been duped. It wasn't the czar; it was court jester Harry Lehr in disguise. Harry henceforth would be known as "King Lehr."

Mrs. Fish always served champagne at dinner. She said wine made guests sleepy and boring. She once had a baby elephant walk through a house party to startle her guests. On another occasion, with the help of Harry Lehr, she kidnapped a socialite's dachshund and covered it with flour from head to toe. The two pranksters then turned their captive loose at the fashionable Newport Casino, where all the ladies that day were wearing black dresses and were soon covered in white flour paw prints. When Mr. and Mrs. Fish

Crossways was Mrs. Stuyvesant Fish's Newport mansion. Mrs. Fish was renowned for her wild and sometimes bizarre parties, including the "dog dinner" held here.

rose to leave a dinner early, Harry Lehr shouted across the room to them, "Sit Down Fishes, you are not rich enough to leave first." This pair was something high society had never seen before.

One summer afternoon, Harry Lehr received word that an old friend named Joseph Leiter was sailing into Newport harbor the next day with an Italian prince onboard. Prince Del Drago was arriving and Harry and his wife Elizabeth would be the hosts for this honored guest. Invitations went out to close friends and word spread around town that an Italian prince was arriving for a visit. The next evening, Joe Lieter arrived with the prince, which turned out to be a pet monkey dressed in formal attire. The monkey prince was seated at the formal table in the seat usually reserved for Mrs. Astor, right between Mrs. Lehr and Mrs. Fish. The servants were warned to keep the prince's champagne consumption to a minimum. Mrs. Lehr commented, "The monkey was well behaved and his behavior compared favorably to other princes I have met." The servants ignored their orders and the prince had several glasses of champagne. The prince eventually climbed atop a chandelier and began tossing light bulbs at the startled guests below. The "monkey dinner," as it would be known, was one of the most famous and bizarre events ever held on Bellevue Avenue.

The enigmatic Mrs. Fish and some of her "accomplices," including architect Stanford White, newspaper editor James Gordon Bennett and comic sidekick Harry Lehr, seated on the floor to the left.

Mrs. Fish's most famous social gathering was the "dog dinner." Bored with the same old people and parties, she decided to hold a function for society's four-legged friends. One hundred pampered canines attended, many in formal attire, and dined on a menu of chopped liver and fricassee of bones served in sterling silver bowls. Mrs. Fish and Harry Lehr had created another party that had all of society talking.

Sometimes, Mrs. Fish was too outrageous for some conservative members of high society. "Old money" Newporter and railroad tycoon James Van Alen was holding a musical in honor of his guest, J.P. Morgan. Harry Lehr's wife Elizabeth was invited, as was Mr. Fish, but the two troublemakers were not. Mrs. Fish rushed over to Bailey's Beach to confront Mr. Van Alen. When she cornered the old man, he told her frankly, "I can't have you and Harry at my party, you two make entirely too much noise." Mrs. Fish did what any good society woman would do: she threatened to spread the rumor that the Van Alen's chef had smallpox. Mr. Van Alen relented if the pair would promise to behave themselves.

One of Mrs. Fish's last great galas was the "Mother Goose ball," in 1913, where all guests attended as fairy tale characters. Mrs. Fish presided over the festivities as the Fairy Queen. Mrs. Fish passed away unexpectedly in 1915, at the age of sixty, of a cerebral hemorrhage at her upstate New York estate. With Mrs. Fish's death, the recently passed income tax amendment and a world war brewing in Europe, conspicuous consumption and the Gilded Age itself would soon be coming to an end.

THE PLAYBOY EDITOR

If there was one man who epitomized the wild partying and no-holds-barred spending of Newport's gilded era, it may have been James Gordon Bennett Jr. Bennett had taken control of his father's newspaper, the *New York Herald*, in 1866. James Gordon Bennett Jr. was a maverick owner/editor who realized early on that sensationalized stories drive newspaper sales. Bennett funded the expedition of Henry Stanley to find the lost Dr. Livingston in Africa in 1869, with the *Herald* having exclusive rights to Stanley's progress. It ended with the phrase, "Doctor Livingston, I presume."

Bennett was flamboyant and cocky in his personal life. He was a yachting enthusiast, becoming the youngest commodore of the New York Yacht Club. Many times, to announce his arrival at a restaurant, he would yank the tablecloths off of other diners' tables on the way to his. He would then hand the waiter some cash to pay for damages and compensate diners for lost meals. Bennett was also known to drink excessively. He caused quite a scandal in 1877, at a party that was held for his engagement to New York socialite Caroline May. After showing up late and drunk, he urinated in the fireplace in front of shocked guests. The wedding was immediately cancelled and Bennett went to Paris to lay low for a while after his unpleasant incident appeared in the *Guinness Book of Records* as the worst engagement faux pas.

While in Paris, Bennett started a European version of his paper called the *International Herald Tribune*. For the new paper, he funded an expedition to the North Pole via the Bering Strait. This expedition did not have the same results as had the search for Dr. Livingston in Africa. The expedition was stranded and twenty members of the group starved to death, although newspaper sales on coverage of the tragedy went through the roof.

Bennett left a lasting mark on Newport, almost by accident, after a bizarre incident. Bennett was an early proponent of polo and was a founding member of the Westchester Polo Club in 1876. Shortly thereafter, he hosted the captain of the British polo team at the exclusive men's club, the Newport Reading Room. Perhaps Bennett was drunk or really bored, but he dared his friend Captain Henry Augustus "Sugar" Candy to ride his horse onto the front porch and into the lobby of the conservative club. Sugar Candy gladly accepted, wildly riding upon to the deck and rearing the horse onto its hind legs. The stodgy club members were mortified and screamed a newly created cliché at Candy: "Get down off your high horse!"

The members banned Candy, forever revoking his guest pass, and strongly censured Bennett. Bennett was outraged; how dare these grumpy old men try to restrict me, he thought. In his anger, he decided to build his own social club. And that's exactly what the fiesty newspaperman did, commissioning architect and good friend Stanford White to build the most elaborate and beautiful club anyone had ever seen. White's creation was known as the Newport Casino, one of the most fashionable locations in all of the city. In its heyday, during the gilded era, the Newport Casino offered a wide array of social diversions to the summer colony including archery, billiards,

An artist's rendering of the incident when maverick newspaper editor James Gordon Bennett dared his drinking buddy Captain Henry Augustus "Sugar" Candy to ride his horse onto the balcony of the exclusive Newport Reading Room; the conservative club members shouted vigorously at Candy, "Get down off your high horse!" *Illustration by Jen Bailey.*

bowling, concerts, dancing, dining, horse shows, lawn bowling, reading, tennis, tea parties and theatricals. It was best known as the home of the newly intoduced lawn tennis; the Casino hosted the national championships from 1881 to 1914, later called the U.S. Open Tennis Championship. (The Casino was not a gambling establishment; it means "little villa" in Italian.) The block-long Bellevue Avenue building is currently home to the International Tennis Hall of Fame. The U.S. Open Championships moved to its present home in Forest Hills, New York.

After a night of reveling, Bennett had the bad habit of driving his team of horses at full speed around the winding roads of Newport. It must have been quite a shock for people who witnessed these wild rides to see Bennett sitting atop his coach, naked as he drove. One of these wild, drunken rides almost changed the course of history. Bennett was entertaining a beautiful young woman from New York named Jenny Jerome, the daughter of a prominent financier. Bennett took the lovely Miss Jerome for a late night carriage ride, this time crashing after taking a turn too quickly and flipping the carriage, ejecting both passengers. Miss Jerome was badly injured but survived and went on to marry Lord Randolph Churchill, becoming the mother of future British Prime Minister Winston Churchill. Who knows how history might have changed if Bennett had accidently killed Miss Jenny Jerome. Would Great Britain have been able to withstand the Nazi onslaught of World War II without the staunch leadership of Winston Churchill?

After James Gordon Bennett's pranks got him reprimanded at the haughty Reading Room, Bennett decided he would have his own private club built. The result was the magnificent Newport Casino, current home of the International Tennis Hall of Fame.

Bennett would continue to collect big-boy toys, especially yachts, building the massive *Lysistrata*, with a crew of one hundred. Bennett's passion for the newspaper business waned into the 1900s and he moved to Paris full time. At the age of seventy-three, he would finally tie the knot, to Baroness de Reuter, daughter of the news agency founder. He passed away in 1918, and his beloved newspaper, the *Herald*, merged with its bitter rival, the *New York Tribune*. Besides the Newport Casino, Bennett left behind memories of a maverick pioneer businessman who preferred to do things his way. Based on his controversial reputation, Bennett left behind an expression that is still used in the British vernacular. When a Brit utters an expression of disbelief, they still reply, "Gordon Bennett." James Gordon Bennett would probably tip his glass and smirk in approval.

THE SWINGER ARCHITECT

S tanford White was one the greatest architects of the late nineteenth and early twentieth centuries. After a short apprenticeship under architect Henry Hobson Richardson and a year-and-a-half-long tour of Europe, Stanford White would return to New York City in 1879. White would join forces with Charles Follen McKim and William Rutherford Mead to form one of the most prolific architectural firms in history. This trio inspired a movement that today is known as the American Renaissance, creating some of this country's grandest structures. McKim, Mead and White would create the massive Pennsylvania Train Station, the Washington Square Arch and the second Madison Square Garden, all in Manhattan. They would also leave their mark on Newport, including the first shingle-style home, the Isaac Bell House, James Gordon Bennett's Casino and their masterpiece, Rosecliff. Rosecliff was completed in 1902 for Teresa Fair Oelrichs, one of society's grand hostesses. Her father, James Fair, had partly discovered the Comstock silver mine in Nevada. Teresa commissioned White to construct a mansion for entertaining. White's creation was inspired by palaces he had seen in Europe and he modeled Rosecliff after the Grand Trianon at Versailles. It features the largest ballroom of all the Newport mansions and has been the featured setting for many Hollywood movies including *The Great Gatsby* and *True Lies*.

But Stanford White had a dark side and it was darker than most people would have ever imagined. He led a double life under the very eyes of his adoring wife, Bessie, who chose not to see but could not fail to suffer from her husband's incessant debauchery. White's scandalous "parties," known for their over-sexed, scantily clad maidens and bubbling French champagne, were often memorialized on the front pages of the tabloids of the day. He was a lavish entertainer with a penchant for young, beautiful women. The more young women, the better for White. White was obsessed with young maidens and it would eventually cost him his life. On the second floor of his tower apartment at Madison Square Garden, a building he designed, a red velvet swing dangled from the gold-leaf ceiling; the tender and agreeable body of one of his infinite girls would often occupy the swing. One such occupant of the notorious red swing was a seventeen-year-old redheaded beauty named Evelyn Nesbit. At sixteen, she had posed for the famous Charles Dana Gibson. At seventeen, she worked as a chorus girl in the Floradora revue, where she caught the roving eye of Stanford White, who soon made her his mistress.

According to Nesbit, their affair started one evening at White's apartment, when he slipped "something" into her champagne. When she awoke on his satin bedcovers a few hours later, he informed her that "now she was his." Despite this ominous start, their affair lasted for quite a while and White took good financial care of both Miss Nesbit and her mother. But Stanford White eventually grew bored of his conquest and moved on to more "virgin" territory. They parted amicably and Nesbit married Henry "Harry" Kendall Thaw, the multimillionaire heir to a railroad and ore fortune from Pittsburgh. Thaw was better known as the "Pittsburgh Idler." Thaw exhibited violent and paranoid behavior that his mother claimed started in the womb. After his expulsion from Harvard, Thaw went on cocaine benders and frequented Broadway shows. That's how he met his future wife.

Thaw was a cruel and temperamental bully with a penchant for dog whips. Many an ex-lover knew the pain of his whip, for Thaw had a reputation for beating up on women, men and defenseless animals. He was used to getting what he wanted, when he wanted it and at any price. He set his sights on Evelyn Nesbit and would not take "no" for an answer. He pursued her endlessly, dazzling her with expensive jewels and finery until she finally accepted his proposal of marriage.

Nesbit's new husband beat her on their honeymoon until she revealed all the details of her former affair with Stanford White. Thaw vowed to get even with the man who "deflowered" his wife. His deadly rage consumed him and finally erupted at the supper club theatre on the roof of Madison Square Garden on the night of June 25, 1906. Concealing a pistol under a heavy overcoat, Thaw followed Stanford White to the opening of the musical *Mam'zelle Champagne*. White was a financial backer of the production. Thaw approached White's table just as the song "I Could Love a Thousand Girls" began to play and fired three shots at close range into his face and head. The crowd thought the gunshots were an elaborate prank, something common for theatrical productions of the time, and didn't react immediately because they thought it was part of the show. That quickly changed when White, mortally wounded, slumped off his chair and fell bleeding to the floor. The once-calm theatre crowd went screaming toward the exits. Thaw then walked calmly toward the elevators with the pistol raised high over his head. When Evelyn Nesbit confronted Thaw, she screamed, "What have you done?" Thaw replied, "I probably saved your life." Ironically, famed architect Stanford White was murdered in a building that he himself had designed just a few years earlier. An autopsy revealed the fifty-three-year-old White may not have lived much longer. His internal organs, especially his liver, were seriously damaged from his hedonistic lifestyle.

Thaw was arrested and held in prison until his murder trial, but continued a lavish lifestyle, having his meals catered by Delmonico's. Newspapers throughout the country called this the "Trial of the Century." The first trial resulted in a hung jury but the second found Thaw not guilty by reason of insanity. Harry K. Thaw was the first person to avoid jail by invoking the insanity defense. Thaw was briefly housed at an asylum but then escaped to Canada for many years. After returning to the United States, he sexually assaulted and buggy-whipped a young boy in 1917. He would spend seven more years in an asylum before being released.

Evelyn Nesbit divorced Harry Thaw, survived several suicide attempts and overcame a heroine addiction. She continued entertaining and eventually managed several speakeasies during Prohibition. In 1955, Hollywood came calling to make a movie about her affair with Stanford White. She served as a technical advisor for *The Girl in The Red Velvet Swing*, starring a young Joan Collins. She would eventually die in a Santa Monica, California nursing home in 1967, at the age of eighty-two.

Titanic

The sinking of the unsinkable ship *Titanic* sent shockwaves throughout the world. Newport was not immune to this terrible tragedy. Some of the most prominent and wealthiest people on the planet had booked passage on the maiden voyage of one of the most luxurious ships ever to sail. When the liner sailed from Southampton, England, on April 10, 1912, the passenger list was a who's who of politics, industry and high society. Included on the passenger list were American industrialist Benjamin Guggenheim, Macy's Department Store owner Isidor Straus and a Denver millionaire socialite named Molly Brown. Also onboard was the White Star Line's chairman, J. Bruce Ismay. On April 11, the ship docked in Cherbourg, France, to board some more first-class passengers, including Colonel John Jacob Astor IV and his new wife Madeline. After a stop in Ireland to pick up mail and third-class passengers, the *Titanic* was on its way to New York and a scheduled arrival on April 17. Banker J.P. Morgan, chocolate man Milton Hershey and railroad heir Alfred Vanderbilt were scheduled to sail on the maiden voyage as well, but all cancelled at the last minute. With Captain Edward John Smith at the controls, the massive ship headed west at twenty-two knots, even though there were iceberg warnings for the North Atlantic. It is believed that Chairman J. Bruce Ismay may have pressured the captain to continue at a high speed to set a record for Atlantic crossing time.

On the evening of April 14, around 11:40 p.m., a lookout spotted a giant iceberg on the starboard side of the ship. Despite the best efforts of the crew and a hard turn to port, the iceberg scraped the bottom of the *Titanic*, ripping holes below the waterline. The watertight doors that were supposed to prevent a sinking did not go high enough to prevent a massive overflow in the case of catastrophic damage. The doors were closed but the damage was so severe that the water flooded over the doors into higher compartments and the ship began to sink, bow first. One hour had passed before the first lifeboat hit the water. The crew assessed the damage before Captain Smith gave the order to evacuate, women and children first. The passengers were unaware that there weren't enough lifeboats for all onboard. Many of the early launches sailed at less than full capacity, the prevailing thought being to remain on a warm ship until rescue boats arrived. After almost two hours, it was clear the *Titanic* was going under and things grew more desperate as men were trying to gang rush the few remaining lifeboats and were held back at gunpoint. One exception to the women and children first rule was White Star chairman J. Bruce Ismay, who survived the sinking on a lifeboat. It is certain his high-ranking position entitled him to a seat, although a rumor spread he had dressed as a woman to avoid the icy water. By 2:20 a.m. on April 15, 1912, the *Titanic* was gone, slipping below the freezing North Atlantic waters in less than three hours. A total of 1,523 people lost their lives, most succumbing to death from hypothermia in the thirty-one-degree water. The human body can only be exposed to these water temperatures for a few minutes before the organs begin to shut down and the victim becomes unconscious. There were fewer than ten passengers pulled from the water that survived, but hundreds were alive and floating where their ship used to be. There was a large black Newfoundland dog that was in the water over three hours and was rescued by the first ship on the scene, the *Carpathia*. Only 306 bodies of the 1,523 victims were ever recovered; 705 lucky people survived. Captain Smith was not one of the lucky ones, going down with his ship. The captain had planned to retire after safely guiding the *Titanic* to New York City.

One of Newport's part-time residents who perished in the *Titanic*'s sinking was George Duncan Widener, who resided most of the year in Philadelphia. Mr. Widener, his wife Eleanor and son Harry were vacationing in Paris and were returning to America aboard the luxury liner. He inherited the Philadelphia Traction Company from his father and oversaw the operation of cable and electric streetcars in Philadelphia as well as in Chicago and New York City. The Widener family decided to vacation in Europe while awaiting the completion of their Newport summer home, Miramar.

Mr. Widener and young son Harry did not survive the sinking and their bodies were never recovered. Mrs. Widener and her maid did survive and Miramar was completed shortly thereafter. Mrs. Widener also had Miramar architect Horace Trumbauer erect the Widener Library at Harvard University in honor of her son, who was a graduate. A popular but unfounded urban legend states that the former requirement that Harvard students pass a swim test in order to graduate was based on Mrs. Widener's stipulation in her bequest. It wasn't that Harry couldn't swim; he likely

The RMS *Titanic* before its maiden voyage from Southampton, England. Two prominent part-time Newport residents as well as another 1,520 people met their end when the luxury liner sank after striking an iceberg April 15, 1912.

froze to death in the icy water. The Miramar mansion is still a private home along prestigious Bellevue Avenue and, in 2006, set a record for the most expensive single-family home price in Rhode Island: $17 million.

By far the wealthiest passenger aboard the *Titanic* was John Jacob Astor IV and his new wife Madeline, who was pregnant with the couple's first child. Astor was the son of William Backhouse and Caroline of high-society fame and the heir to a vast real estate and hotel fortune. John Jacob Astor IV was not considered to be the smartest businessman and was certainly fortunate to have such a great inheritance. He had also had some terrible luck with boats, once running his yacht aground on a sandbar and, in another incident, he rammed the Vanderbilt yacht *North Star* off of Newport. The society press

Miramar was built for the Widener family of Philadelphia. Mrs. Widener suggested a cruise aboard the *Titanic* while waiting for the summer cottage to be completed. In 2006, Miramar set the record for highest single-family home price in Rhode Island at just over $17 million.

poked fun at these foul-ups, nicknaming him "Jackass." Astor was no stranger to summering in Newport. He had rented many Bellevue Avenue mansions until inheriting his mother's social headquarters, Beechwood, after her death in 1908. After his mother's death, Astor also got a divorce from a prearranged marriage, to Philadelphia socialite Ava Willing, set up by his mother. Ava sued for divorce on the grounds of adultery in 1909 and John Jacob did not contest—they both wanted out of this marriage. This paved the way for the forty-seven-year-old "Colonel" Astor (as he preferred to be called) to marry the eighteen-year-old Madeline Talmage Force on September 9, 1911, in the ballroom at Beechwood. (In an attempt to rehabilitate his public image, Astor outfitted his own company of artillerymen during the Spanish-American War. He also donated his yacht *Nourmahal* to the navy and a battery of howitzer cannons to the army. He saw brief service in the field in Cuba.) The wedding almost did not take place at all. Since Astor was an admitted adulterer, no priest in good conscience would perform the ceremony. Astor essentially bribed a Providence clergyman $1,000 to perform the nuptials. The couple then hurried off to Europe to let things cool down at home. In April 1912, the couple decided to return to the States so the baby could be born at home. What better way to return than the inaugural transatlantic sail aboard the *Titanic*?

As the ship started to sink, Colonel Astor put his pregnant wife in one of the lifeboats and assured her that with calm seas, she would be fine. He waved goodbye as the boat was lowered and told her he would see her tomorrow. But tomorrow would never come for the Colonel. He tried to keep his cool and even joked to fellow passengers, "I asked for ice in my drink, but this is ridiculous." A week later, the grim task of recovering bodies went to the ship *Mackay-Bennett*. Astor's body was recovered, bobbing upright in his lifebelt. His gold watch and $2,500 in cash were found in his blue suit's pocket. The body was partially crushed and covered in soot. Astor may have been killed when the large smokestack collapsed on deck, just before the ship's final plunge. His corpse was shipped to Halifax and then to New York for burial in the Astor plot. Madeline did survive the sinking and on August 14, 1912, she gave birth to a son who was named John Jacob Astor VI in honor of his father. (There was already a John Jacob Astor V, born to cousin and business rival William Waldorf Astor.) Madeline would inherit income from a $5 million trust fund under the stipulation that she did not remarry. When she remarried in 1916, she lost her stipend and use of a Fifth Avenue mansion. Madeline would die at the relatively young age of forty-six in Palm Beach, Florida, of a heart ailment. She never spoke publicly about the sinking. She did once mention to a friend that her last recollection of the *Titanic* was seeing their pet, Airedale, pacing the ship's deck, just before it sank.

Part-time Newport resident and the wealthiest passenger aboard the *Titanic*, John Jacob Astor IV, and new wife, Madeline, go for a stroll. Astor's $100 million fortune couldn't save him from dying in the icy North Atlantic.

John Jacob IV's son, Vincent, instantly became one of the wealthiest people alive with the sinking of the *Titanic*. Vincent was Astor's son from his first marriage to Ava Willing. His estimated inheritance was over $200 million. After his father's death, he dropped out of Harvard and went on a philanthropic campaign. Over time, he sold off the family's New York City slum housing and reinvested in reputable enterprises while spending a great deal of time and energy helping others. He was responsible for the construction of a large housing complex in the Bronx that included sufficient land for a large children's playground; in Harlem, he transformed a valuable piece of real estate into another playground for children. In 1953, Vincent married for the third time, this time to a woman named Brooke. Upon Astor's death in 1959, Brooke inherited the entire Astor fortune. Her death, in 2007, has also been extremely controversial and scandalous. There have been accusations of will tampering and elder abuse made against her son and his attorney. It is almost inevitable that dark clouds gather over these large family fortunes. When such vast amounts of money are involved, there will no doubt be vultures circling to lay their claim to an inheritance they have no stake in. Greed almost always trumps compassion when these families fight over inheritance.

LVSITANIA

On the morning of April 15, 1912, when news of the *Titanic*'s sinking hit the East Coast of America, Alfred Gwynne Vanderbilt must have felt like one of the luckiest men alive. He had booked passage on the ship's maiden voyage, but a last-minute business meeting forced him to rearrange his plans. Alfred Vanderbilt, it seemed, always had luck on his side. His oldest brother William, certain heir to the family fortune, died of typhoid fever while attending Yale in 1892. His older brother "Neily" was disinherited by his parents, Cornelius II and Alice, because he married a women with a questionable reputation. That left Alfred next in line for the jackpot and in 1899, when his father passed away, he became a wealthy man of leisure.

Alfred never really liked working in the railroad business; he preferred to spend his time breeding championship racehorses. His large Oakland Farm estate was just up the road from Newport in nearby Portsmouth. Alfred looked the part of a wealthy gentleman, always impeccably dressed in expensive suits and his signature top hat; he was described as handsome and dashing. Alfred also had a weakness for beautiful young women, whether they were married or not. His first wife, Ellen French, filed for divorce after discovering an affair between Alfred and Agnes Ruiz, the wife of a Cuban ambassador. The public humiliation and scandal caused Ruiz to commit suicide in 1909. Alfred was remarried in London to a wealthy divorcée, Margaret Emerson McKim, in 1911. But marriage did not stop Alfred's womanizing ways.

When Alfred Vanderbilt stepped aboard the *Lusitania* on May 1, 1915, his luck was running out. It was rumored that someone had slipped a note under his hotel door the night before departure, warning him that the ship would be attacked. He obviously felt the note was a hoax. He wasn't going to miss this trip. He was on his way to a meeting of the International Horse

Alfred Vanderbilt inspects his car before it is loaded into the *Lusitania*'s hold. It is possible that war munitions in the hold may have expedited the ship's sinking.

The *Lusitania*'s sinking also ended the life of a wealthy Newport heir. Alfred Vanderbilt was a passenger on the torpedoed cruise ship that sank less than eight miles from the Irish coast in eighteen minutes. Here is a look at "Lucy," docked in New York City.

Breeder's Association, and could not miss it as the previous year's meeting had been cancelled due to the outbreak of war. He was traveling with his personal valet and a mistress. None of the passengers heeded the notice advertised in the *New York Times* on April 22, warning that a state of war existed between Great Britain and Germany:

> *Notice! Travelers intending to embark on the Atlantic voyage are reminded that a state of war exists between Germany and her allies and Great Britain and her allies; that the zone of war includes the waters adjacent to the British Isles; that, in accordance with formal notice given by the Imperial German Government, vessels flying the flag of Great Britain, or any of her allies, are liable to destruction in those waters and that travelers sailing in the war zone on ships of Great Britain or her allies do so at their own risk.*

> *Imperial German Embassy; Washington D.C.*

The notice appeared on the same page that advertised the *Lusitania*'s scheduled departure from New York. Unlike the *Titanic*, which sank on its maiden voyage, *Lusitania* was a veteran of North Atlantic crossings. She had been making scheduled trips between New York and Liverpool since 1907, with 201 crossings without incident. The ship's captain, William Turner, had been at sea since the age of thirteen. A submarine attack was one of his last concerns. Even operating without all boilers to conserve valuable coal, which was scarce during wartime, Captain Turner was sure he could outrun any U-boat the Germans had. He loathed his duties as a "Cunard Ambassador" to the rich and powerful who frequently sailed his ship. This included nearly all of the first-class passengers on any given voyage. Captain Turner found foul weather to be a savior as it kept him on the bridge and away from the annoyances of pointless questions about the ship's functions or petty complaints about the sauce served with the previous evening's meal. He had a ship, its passengers and a crew to deliver safely to England. The *Lusitania* departed two hours late from New York harbor because three German spies were found onboard and were detained below deck, certainly an ominous sign for this voyage.

On May 5 and 6, the German submarine U-20, commanded by Kapitänleutnant Walther Schwieger, was hunting merchant vessels off the southern Irish coast, sinking three. The British Royal Navy had sent submarine warnings to all British ships in the area and the *Lusitania* did receive them as well, even though she was flying the American flag. According to rules of engagement at the time, U-boats could only sink merchant ships after allowing the crew to abandon ship and only after boarding and discovering contraband war materials. Captain Turner took prudent precautions, closing the watertight doors, posting double lookouts, ordering a blackout and swinging the lifeboats away from the ship's side. That way if they were torpedoed, the boats could launch quickly. Captain Turner also headed northeast toward the Irish coast, assuming U-boats would be in deeper waters and not along the coastline. On May 7, U-20 was low on fuel and had only three torpedoes left, so Commander Schwieger headed for Germany. At this point, the *Lusitania* was only forty miles from the Head of Old Kinsale when heavy fog rolled in and slowed their speed to a perilous eighteen knots. Just as the U-20 hit full speed toward German waters, Captain Schwieger saw a dark silhouette on the horizon, steaming right toward him. Captain Schwieger gave the order to fire one torpedo as the *Lusitania* passed, but quartermaster Charles Voegele refused to fire. He was eventually court-martialed for disobeying a direct order and spent three years in prison. Voegele knew the ship was a passenger liner and refused to attack innocent women and children. When the torpedo was launched it was a direct hit near the bow, almost below the bridge, smashing a massive hole in the metal plates and sending a huge plume of debris skyward.

An SOS was sent and Captain Turner issued an immediate order to abandon ship. Water flooded the ship's starboard compartments, causing an immediate fifteen-degree starboard tilt. Captain Turner tried turning the ship toward the Irish coast in the hope of beaching her, but the helm would not respond. The torpedo had knocked out the steam lines to the rudder, rendering the controls useless. The ship's propellers continued to drive the ship at eighteen knots, forcing water into her hull. As the ship listed, many of the lifeboats were useless. Some were swung too far out to board while others were banging against the ship's side. It was absolute chaos on the decks. Within six minutes of the torpedo hitting the *Lusitania*, the water had almost reached the top decks. Many survivors also reported a second explosion, which they thought was a second torpedo. While it is certain the *Lusitania* was carrying war materiel and maybe even small-arms ammunition, these were not the cause of the second large explosion. It was caused by a large coal dust cloud igniting after being stirred up in the near empty coal bunkers. This second explosion ripped more plates off the side of the wounded liner, expediting the inevitable. By this time, passengers were just leaping off the wounded ship to take their chances in the Irish Sea. Captain Turner would stay on the bridge under the floor that was flooded out from under his feet. The captain would survie after three hours in the water by clinging to a deck chair.

Since Alfred Vanderbilt's body was never found, there are numerous memorials dedicated to his honor, including these anchors and fountain on Broadway in Newport. There is also a large plaque and stained-glass window to Alfred's memory inside Trinity Church. *Photo courtesy of the author.*

Lusitania sank in only eighteen minutes, less than eight miles from the Old Head of Kinsale, Ireland. (Ironically, Kinsale is a sister city of Newport.) Of the 1,959 passengers to leave New York, 1,198 did not survive the attack; 128 of the victims were Americans. After massive international outcry, Captain Schwieger was considered a war criminal and later, in 1915, the kaiser ended unresticted submarine warfare altogether. There was speculation at the time of the sinking that America would immediately enter the war on the British side to avenge those killed. Some people even speculated the British navy, including First Lord of the Admiralty Winston Churchill, did send escort ships to guide the *Lusitania* through U-boat–infested waters. The British had assumed if the liner was attacked, it would force America to enter the fray. President Woodrow Wilson was determined to keep Americans out of the fighting across the European continent. Even after the sinking he resisted before commiting troops in 1917.

Despite a $1,000 reward for his body, Alfred Vanderbilt was never found. Some survivors say Alfred had given his life vest to a young mother and her infant child when she could not locate one. It is even rumored he tied the vest on her, with her baby in her arms, just before water swept over the decks. This was a heroic and gallant move by Alfred. Despite being a noted sportsman, he had never learned to swim, and probably knew he would die. Tragedy had once again come to the house of Vanderbilt. There are momuments to Alfred's memory in Newport, including a fountain with anchors on either side off of Broadway as well as a plaque inside Trinity Church.

THE COURT JESTER'S SECRET

Harry Lehr never quite measured up. He survived a premature birth weight and low self-esteem to become the court jester and class clown of Newport's late gilded era. Lehr was born into an upper-middle-class family in Baltimore yet always wanted to be included in the upper crust. His dreams took a serious detour when his merchant father committed suicide after a financial panic in 1886. Harry moved to Paris to try his hand at banking but he realized he did not care for work. Harry returned to New York City and made his way as a social climber. Harry was flamboyant, charismatic and at ease at cocktail parties, working the room like a wealthy gentleman of leisure. Harry Lehr quickly learned he could make a living by being himself. Being able to crack a joke and being a quick wit and expert piano player made Lehr a must-have at New York's numerous parties. Harry was in high demand. He also received endorsement money to promote products at these parties, from champagne to caviar to fine cigars. Upscale New York restaurants gave free dinners to him so gossip would spread that Harry Lehr ate there, hopefully increasing the patronage from high society. He also did something, in 1895, which had never been done before. Harry Lehr convinced Mrs. Astor to join him for dinner at a new Fifth Avenue restaurant. This was the first time she had ever dined in public and ensured Harry free meals there for life. Harry was often sought out by women for fashion advice and was known to be highly critical if he didn't care for an outfit. Life was good for "King Lehr."

Harry's life would change forever when he was introduced to the Queen of Society, Mrs. Astor, at a Newport ball. Harry would assume the role previously held by Ward McAllister as a social advisor and party escort. Lehr would soon be planning all of Mrs. Astor's balls, including hiring caterers and bands for these grand events. But Harry was no Ward McAllister. McAllister was like a ringmaster of a three-ring circus; he felt

The wedding photo of the once-happy couple, Elizabeth Drexel and Harry Lehr. Lehr was able to keep a dark secret from his wife throughout his entire life.

society was a circus and must be managed like one. Lehr was more like the head clown spraying water out of a phony flower on his lapel.

Harry was also introduced to a lovely widow at a Newport ball named Elizabeth Wharton Drexel, heiress to a Philadelphia banking fortune. There was an instant attraction and Harry asked the beautiful Elizabeth to be his wife. But she first had to receive the approval of some of Harry's influential friends. Elizabeth was interviewed over lunch by Mrs. Astor, Alva Belmont, Mrs. Stuyvesant Fish and Teresa Fair Oelrichs—all the grand dames of Newport society. They all felt Elizabeth was lovely and worthy of marrying Harry. The nuptials took place in June 1901. The night of the wedding Harry dropped a bomb on poor Elizabeth. He revealed he had only married her because of her vast wealth and he wanted to be comfortable. Marrying her would cement his place in society and he would be cordial to her in public. In private, he would be insulting and cruel. Worst of all, he refused to have sex with her. Elizabeth was duped. Divorce was out of the question because of her stubborn, Catholic mother, so Elizabeth stayed in an unconsummated marriage for twenty-eight years. Harry went on in his marriage of convenience, clowning it up for the social elite.

With his society patron Mrs. Astor in decline, Harry hooked his wagon to another of Newport's famous party givers, Mrs. Fish. This dynamic duo was made for each other. They were certainly an odd couple. Harry was tall, handsome, charming and looked the part of an aristocrat. Mrs. Fish was somewhat frumpy and would be considered big boned. Harry Lehr frequently joked about her non-feminine features, stating sarcastically she sometimes pretended to be a woman. They were both bored from the same old social gatherings, so they sought new ways to inject a little fun into boring old high society. Numerous themed costume parties as well as practical jokes and animal guests emerged from the twisted minds of this pair. Newport society would never be the same, but many hard-liners did not find them humorous.

With Mrs. Fish's passing in 1915, Harry and Elizabeth Lehr moved to Paris. To keep her mind off of her counterfeit marriage, Elizabeth worked with the Red Cross, caring for World War I casualties. The couple remained in Paris, eventually purchasing a small hotel in 1923. Harry Lehr had quieted down and showed symptoms of depression before the war, which finally put an end to his entertaining. He grew more and more miserable; his mind slowly failed and he became panic-stricken at the thought of his wife leaving him. She accepted an impossible situation, gave him money and buried herself in her war work. Upon Harry's death in 1929, from a brain tumor, he left her his debts as one last spiteful joke. Elizabeth also found his diary and finally realized why her amusing, ostentatious and deceitful husband was the way he was. Harry Lehr was gay.

CURSE OF THE PHARAOHS

If you look at a map of Newport, you will notice the southern tip of the city has a small hook to its geography and has been called "the boot," similar to Italy's. It is hard to believe that an Egyptian curse may have doomed this region, but a strange set of circumstances points to that conclusion.

Originally, this area was granted to a Newport founder and colonial surveyor named William Brenton after 1639. Because the family was so pro-British during the Revolution, the land was confiscated and redistributed to other colonial families after the conflict. The curse may have come from a man who made this area his estate. Theodore M. Davis was a local attorney who also happened to own copper mines and collect rare art. It was his other hobby that jinxed this locale; Mr. Davis was the leading Egyptologist of his time. Mr. Davis had a huge, stone Queen Anne villa, called the Reef, constructed on this site in 1885, with commanding views of the entrance to Newport harbor and the east passage of Narragansett Bay.

Mr. Davis summered on the Nile River in Egypt from 1903 to 1912, and received a rare license from the Egyptian government to excavate the area known as "the Valley of Kings." His excavation team discovered the tombs of Pharaoh Yuya and his wife, as well as the looted tomb of Horemheb. Davis also uncovered some artifacts of Tutankhamen, but in 1912, he declared the valley was fully explored and would yield no more finds. In 1922, archaeologist Howard Carter would prove him wrong with the unearthing of Tutankhamen's tomb. The legend said that anyone who disturbed these sacred tombs would be cursed forever.

The Reef had a large wooden windmill on the estate to supply power and run the pumps in the large stable behind the main house. The stable was known as "the Bells" because of its numerous chimes at the top of the building. After Davis returned from the Valley of the Kings, the windmill was struck by lightning and burned to the ground, making the estate

The Reef was built for wealthy industrialist Theodore M. Davis in 1885. Mr. Davis led numerous expeditions to Egypt and might have been cursed for disturbing a pharaoh's sacred burial plot. *Photo courtesy of the Preservation Society of Newport County.*

A fire that started in this windmill after it was struck by lightning may have been a result of the pharaoh's curse. Currently, there is an observation deck atop the ruins with expansive views of the former estate and the entrance to Narragansett Bay. *Photo courtesy of the author.*

After years of neglect and vandalism, the Reef was finally demolished in 1963, and the State of Rhode Island converted the property into a state park. Visible are the former walls of the Reef as well as the gatehouse, which is still intact. *Photo courtesy of the author.*

uninhabitable. Eventually, the windmill was replaced with a stone structure, but Mr. Davis died before its completion in 1915.

The eighteen-acre property was eventually purchased in 1923, by a prominent Providence car dealer named Milton Budlong, but he and his family would never live on the property. The Budlongs became embroiled in a nasty divorce and the mansion was only used sparingly by family members until 1941. The army took control of the property for use as a coastal defense fortress and antiaircraft guns lined the estate grounds. Gunnery personnel lived in the Reef throughout the war. The Budlongs never returned to the mansion and it remained empty throughout the 1950s. The Reef was heavily vandalized and a large fire finished off the property in 1961. In 1963, citing public safety concerns, the State of Rhode Island took control of the property and demolished the main house. The area was renamed Brenton Point State Park and was opened to the public in 1976. The park is a popular picnicking and kite-flying area today. The large gate house, which serves as public bathrooms, as well as the ruins of the windmill and the stable still remain. If you walk the grounds, you can still see the outline of the Reef, but be careful. You don't want to take the pharaoh's curse back home with you.

BE CAREFUL WHAT YOU

WISH FOR...

Newporters can occasionally be tough to outsiders. Perhaps it's their opposition to change or just their New England distrust of people new to the area. Maybe it's just the native's mentality and suspicion of anyone who wasn't born on the island. Whatever the case may be, Alexander Anderson found out what a tough crowd they really are on July 16, 1907. It seems Alexander Anderson was having a bad day. His wife had left him to return to Boston with their two small children, after having him arrested for a previous assault. He was also fired that morning from his job as a gardener at a nearby estate. So Anderson, as he had done on many previous occasions, got drunk. He then booked a room on the top floor of the Perry House Hotel in Washington Square, just below the Old Colony House and the Newport County Courthouse. (The hotel was razed in the 1920s but stood next to the Opera House Theatre.) The hotel clerk later noted Anderson was acting erratically and reeked of booze when he checked in. About an hour after checked in, someone alerted the clerk that there was a man on the top ledge of the hotel, threatening to jump. The police were summoned and a crowd of about a hundred people gathered in the square below.

While the police had broken down the hotel room door and attempted to coax Anderson back inside the room, the crowd below was becoming unruly and wanted action. Every time the police would venture onto the ledge, Anderson would put his foot off the side, threatening to fall seventy-five feet to the ground below. The crowd wasn't helping matters much, with occasional chants of "Jump, Jump" and "Hurry Up and Do It." Finally, the fire department was called and a ladder was placed up the side of the hotel. The firemen also attempted to get rescue nets in place before Anderson could leap.

A Newport gardener named Alexander Anderson leaped from the top of the Perry House Hotel, shown here in an artist's rendering, giving the chanting crowd exactly what they asked for. According to Ghost Tours of Newport, Rhode Island, Anderson's ghost may still haunt the Washington Square Area. *Illustration by Jen Bailey.*

As the crowd's wishes grew louder and Anderson became more desperate, the police knew something must be done. They attempted to grab Anderson's leg, but he eluded their grasp. Alexander Anderson would give the crowd what they wanted: he leaped off the top-floor ledge of the Perry House Hotel. Witnesses described his descent position as flat, with arms extended as he hurtled toward the ground.

The crowd, which had chanted for Anderson to jump, shrieked in horror as he made his leap, then cried out in revulsion when his body hit the ground. People in the crowd were disgusted when the impact occurred and they could hear Anderson's bones break as he crashed into the street. Some appalled onlookers picked up Anderson's badly bruised body and carried it into a drugstore across the square, while waiting for the ambulance to arrive. When he reached the hospital, there was little doctors could do for the man and he passed away that evening around 5:30 p.m.

A sad end to poor Alexander Anderson. Or was it? According to Ghost Tours of Newport, Mr. Anderson may still be with us, at least in spirit. One of the more active hauntings on their Old Town ghost walk is the very spot where Anderson departed this life. Ghost guides and guests report strange temperature drops, spot glowing orbs and occasionally hear muffled screams from high above Washington Square. According to Ghost Tours of Newport, Anderson may be a residual haunting, which is similar to a film clip being replayed over and over again. When Anderson died, his energy may have been imprinted onto this clip to continue playing for all eternity, in the very spot where a tough Newport crowd gathered to chant for his demise.

PAINT IT BLACK

In a town that has had its fair share of eccentrics and generally bizarre characters, there is one woman who stood head and shoulders above the rest. Her name was Beatrice Turner. Beatrice, born in 1888, was the only daughter of wealthy Philadelphia cotton broker Andrew Turner and his wife Adele. As much as Andrew was a successful businessman, he was also a spiritualist, often writing poetry and interpreting his dreams. He was also overly defensive of his only child. From a young age, Beatrice showed a great talent for painting and was even accepted to the prestigious Pennsylvania Academy of Fine Arts and hoped to one day continue her studies in Europe. This elite schooling was abruptly terminated when her overprotective father discovered his young daughter had been painting nudes. Andrew had some fatherly advice for young Beatrice. She should refocus her considerable talent on painting family members and even portraits of herself. This was advice that she would really take to heart.

About the same time, in 1907, the Turners purchased the former Newport estate of a Maryland governor, high above the beautiful cliff walk, and renamed it Arcadia. But even in Newport, Beatrice could not escape the watchful eye of father Andrew. She was chastised for even walking with a member of the opposite sex along the cliff walk. It seemed Andrew Turner wanted Beatrice all to himself. He expressed some of his unfatherly thoughts in one of his many poems:

> *When look at thy form devine*
> *Perfect in each curve and line*
> *And gazing at they silken hair*
> *And basking in they orbits rare*
> *A misnomer 'twas in naming thee*
> *Aught else but Venus*

There were even considerable rumors that Andrew had repeatedly sexually abused his young daughter, and her future behavior may prove these rumors to be true. In 1913, Andrew returned to Philadelphia to open the family's brownstone for the spring. He was found dead there the next day. Beatrice was devastated and would never be the same. A poem was found in the Philadelphia townhouse that influenced Beatrice to do something bizarre:

I dreamed I dwelt in a house of black
Located in the land of Arcadia
And absolutely nothing did it lack
For I was with my two sweethearts

I awoke and found I was in a house of brown
Far from loving glances and melodious voices
O when we are so far from those that we love
Don't such dreams last until we meet again?

Obviously, the house of brown was the family's brownstone in Philadelphia, so Beatrice interpreted the poem to mean Arcadia was the Newport home. She had it painted funeral black, just like her father instructed. It remained that way until the day she died.

Beatrice would not allow her deceased father to be buried for days; she propped him up in bed until she could finish his portrait. Beatrice would mourn her father for the rest of her life, constantly wearing Victorian clothing and always black. Her neighbors in Newport reported she even wore black while performing simple household chores, like mowing the lawn or raking leaves. And she would continue to paint, at a prolific pace, for the rest of her reclusive life. Beatrice would never marry but would be seen occasionally, walking as a shadowy, solitary figure along the cliff walk below her darkened mansion.

When Beatrice died in 1948, she had no heirs, so the house was sold and its contents were discarded. It was finally revealed what Beatrice had done with all her time. She painted. The house contained over three thousand works of art; a thousand of these were self-portraits of the artist herself. The new owners did not want the artwork, so it was carted off to the town dump and tossed onto a massive bonfire. A lifetime of Beatrice's work was set ablaze. A neighbor was able to salvage a couple of paintings and some passersby took a few as well, but the majority of these masterpieces were incinerated. When the present owner purchased Arcadia in 1989, he made it his mission to restore the property to its former glory and honor

The reclusive Beatrice Turner had her beautiful Newport home, Arcadia (shown here in an artist's rendering), painted black after interpreting her late father's dream journals. The home is now a luxury bed-and-breakfast. *Illustration by Jen Bailey.*

its most eccentric owner. He tracked down as much of Beatrice's surviving artwork as he could find and the relocated pieces now hang throughout the exquisitely restored mansion. Currently, the property is known as the Cliffside Inn, and is one of Newport's most luxurious bed-and-breakfasts.

Beatrice Turner's legacy will always be a part of Newport lore. She will forever be remembered as the talented, reclusive artist whose flower was never allowed to bloom because of her overbearing and abusive father. Her surviving paintings are a sad reminder of what might have become of Beatrice Turner had she been allowed to pursue her true passion.

ANCHORS AWAY

Newport was a navy town. Actually, all of southern Narragansett Bay, both the east and west shores, derived much of its economic base from naval activity. This entire region was dependant on Department of Defense spending for both military and civilian employment. But a decision—influenced by a former, paranoid and vindictive U.S. president—changed this region's economic future forever.

Newport's naval tradition dates all the back to 1775 when the Rhode Island general assembly created the first navy in the western hemisphere. Narragansett Bay was nicknamed "the Cradle of the American Navy." John Paul Jones, often considered the father of the American Navy, captained his first ship in these waters. His sloop the *Providence* would hunt for the HMS *Rose* to end the blockade that had stifled trade among these coastal communities.

The Newport-born and -raised Perry brothers were two of America's early naval heroes. Oliver Hazard Perry was best known for his bravery during the War of 1812. During the Battle of Lake Erie, Perry was able to defeat a British flotilla and secure the Great Lakes. When his report was sent to his superior officer, General William Henry Harrison, the dispatch became Perry's most famous quotation: "We have met the enemy and they are ours."

His brother Matthew Calbraith Perry was a distinguished captain, eventually gaining the rank of commodore, and is credited with modernizing the navy in the 1840s. Perry oversaw the transition from sail to steam power and America's growing role as a world power led by a strong navy. Matthew C. Perry's most famous mission was as an envoy of President Millard Fillmore. In 1852, he led an expedition of warships to Japan. Perry's mission was to open Japan to trade with the west, a privilege that only the Dutch enjoyed. Perry would not take "no" for an answer. If Japanese officials would not oblige, Perry would be forced to bombard their cities with his superior military force. The Japanese reluctantly agreed because they feared the firepower of Perry's black ships. In 1854, the Kanagawa Treaty officially opened Imperial Japan to trade with the west. An annual festival called Black Ships—celebrated between Newport and sister city Shimodo, in Japan—commemorates Perry's mission of peace by force.

Newport's navy tradition continued into the Civil War when the U.S. Naval Academy was relocated to the Atlantic House Hotel on Bellevue Avenue and away from Confederate forces and hostilities close to Annapolis, Maryland. The USS *Constitution*, "Old Ironsides," was docked at Fort Adams in Newport for safekeeping during the War Between the States.

After the Civil War, the Naval War College was established in Newport, in 1885, on the site of the former asylum for the poor on Coaster's Harbor Island. The navy also established a training station for recruits and a torpedo-development facility and factory on Goat Island. The war college has long been an important teaching facility of top navy personnel and an important location for planning strategic naval policy. Newport was becoming an important city in the navy's strategic plan for defense of the world's oceans.

The peak of Newport's naval prominence came during World War II, when there were over 162,000 personnel deployed throughout the area. The state's largest employer at this time was the torpedo factory on Goat Island, where 14,000 people worked around the clock in three shifts to supply the navy with torpedoes for the war effort. Over 90 percent of these projectiles used during the war were produced right here in Newport. On the west side of Narragansett Bay was Naval Air Station Quonset, which is where the first radar-equipped night fighters were tested, before their deployment over Europe. Davisville was home to the Seabees, a naval construction battalion, who were responsible for quickly constructing airstrips, especially on small Pacific islands. North of Newport was the PT boat–training facility at Melville, where a young ensign named John F. Kennedy was put through his paces before commanding the ill-fated PT-109. The Newport area did all it could to support the fight for freedom.

After World War II, Newport continued as an important home port for much of the navy's Atlantic fleet. The Cruiser-Destroyer command would remain in the city's waters, which meant over one hundred capital ships called the Newport area home. If you ask old navy veterans what they remember about their time in Newport, many of them will tell you the same thing: the bars. The city's waterfront and downtown catered to the sailors on leave, with dozens of bars, tattoo parlors and brothels lining the streets. Old salts speak longingly of Leo's First and Last Stop, which stood at the end of

The U.S. Navy had a presence in the Newport area beginning soon after the Revolutionary War and continuing throughout the early 1970s. The large Cruiser-Destroyer fleet was headquartered here as well, making Newport a busy port of call. *Photo courtesy of Department of the Navy—Naval Historical Center.*

Long Wharf. This coincidently was the drop-off point for the navy's tender boats, ferrying sailors from the nearby Destroyer piers on their way to liberty in Newport. Other favorites were the Blue Moon on Thames Street and the notorious bars along Blood Alley. Only the toughest sailors dared to venture here. Blood Alley got its nickname because the street flowed with blood after the numerous fights and stabbings between rowdy seamen and tough local fishermen. The shore patrol and their paddy wagons were always close by to round up sailors who misbehaved and transport them to the brig.

All this would change in 1973. The Vietnam War had ended. Military spending was declining. Rumors were flying throughout Newport and Washington, D.C., that the navy's presence would be coming to an end. City officials were scrambling to fill the monetary void that a navy departure would create. Locals were panicked: how would the millions of military dollars be replaced? Many economic consultants recommended to the local government to turn its attention to attracting newly formed high-tech companies like International Business Machines to move to Rhode Island if the navy decided to move to another location. But local government officials had different ideas. They decided tourism was the way to go. Local government would turn its attention to developing Newport into a major tourism center. Many experts scoffed at the idea, pointing out that the area beaches could not accommodate large groups of tourists and the peak season would last just two months. But local officials would not budge. If the navy left Newport high and dry, the economy would become driven by tourism.

Newport received the bad news in early 1973. An economic commission recommended the Quonset air station to be decommissioned and the Cruiser-Destroyer command to be transferred to Norfolk, Virginia. Only the Naval War College and other instructional schools would remain. Thousands of naval personnel and civilian jobs were gone, along with the money spent in the local economy.

The Department of Defense insisted that these cuts were strictly based on strategic decisions and were not politically motivated. But many locals were quick to disagree. If you had asked a local businessperson who depended on the navy for their livelihood who was responsible for the cutback, there would be a common response: President Richard Nixon was to blame. Nixon won the 1972 election over George McGovern in a landslide and carried every state except Massachusetts. Rhode Island, which is traditionally Democrat, voted for Nixon but just barely; he garnered a little over 50 percent of the vote. If the Newport navy base closed, the Boston Shipyard would also fold, and the jobs and military spending would flow to Virginia, an area that had strongly supported Nixon's reelection. Many locals felt Nixon was punishing the Democratic Northeast for not supporting him completely. History has shown President Nixon was not above taking revenge upon his political rivals whenever he felt it was warranted. Although it was never officially disclosed, other than for strategic military purposes, the redeployment of the large Cruiser-Destroyer fleet was Nixon's sarcastic thank-you for a lack of political support throughout the region. But whatever the reason, Newport had to scramble to keep its economy afloat.

The downtown area was redeveloped with a large four-lane road cutting through the Old Point neighborhood to deliver tourists directly to the waterfront. Government Landing, the downtown pier for visiting dignitaries, was developed into a waterfront hotel. Even the old torpedo factory was razed and Goat Island became the home of a luxury hotel and resort. The old wharf area, previously home to the seedy and dangerous Blood Alley bars, was sanitized for tourists and now contains upscale shops and

The submarine *Tarantula* is put through its paces, in 1907, in Newport harbor. Goat Island, now home to a luxury hotel, was the location of the largest torpedo factory in the country. Notice the Rose Island lighthouse in the distance. *Photo courtesy of Department of the Navy— Naval Historical Center.*

waterfront restaurants. Newport had made an amazing transformation and would be almost unrecognizable to an old navy seaman who, at one time, wandered the downtown streets on leave. For better or for worse, Newport is now a tourist town. Like every tourist town, Newport has some minor problems, like lack of parking and long waits at restaurants in the summer. But if you consider the positives—like the beautiful harbor front, the quaint colonial streets and the amazing architecture, from pre-Revolutionary homes to gilded-era mansions—Newport has a lot to offer. It seems a shame that such local treasures would not have been available to both tourists and locals had the navy remained entrenched in the area. So President Nixon actually did those of us who enjoy Newport's charm and beauty a big favor after all. Thank you, Mr. President.

THE RICHEST GIRL
IN THE WORLD

Whoever coined the phrase "You can never be too rich or too thin" probably never heard of Doris Duke. When Doris was born on November 22, 1912, she was called the richest girl in the world. Her father, James Buchanan Duke, founded the American Tobacco Company in Durham, North Carolina, and had a true rags-to-riches story. His family's farm was destroyed during the Civil War and he restarted the crops from a few salvaged tobacco seeds. Mr. Duke was the first manufacturer to implement a cigarette-rolling machine. This new technology gave American Tobacco a huge advantage over its competitors, and their Lucky Strike cigarettes were one of the most popular brands in America. American Tobacco was the first major company to use scantily clad women to promote its products. Mr. Duke also wisely invested some of the cigarette profits into supplying much of the rural South with electricity. Mr. Duke's foresight would grow to become Duke Energy and Southern Company, which generates electricity from hydroelectric power. These wise decisions would ensure that the Duke fortune would last for generations. Mr. Duke was also very generous with his money, donating a large endowment to the small Trinity University in Durham. If you have never heard of Trinity, you're not alone. The school was renamed Duke University in the generous benefactor's honor.

Doris was the only child of James and his second wife Nanoline Holt, a true Southern aristocrat. Doris was the apple of her father's eye and had only a lukewarm relationship with her mother. She truly was her daddy's girl. In 1925, her beloved father unexpectedly fell ill with pneumonia. The story goes that his scheming wife, Nanoline, wanted him dead, so she kept the windows in their Fifth Avenue mansion open so the freezing cold air would speed his demise and Nanoline could garner her inheritance. However, Nanoline's scheme failed. James did die, but most of his money went to

Doris. Nanoline only received use of the family homes until her death. When James Duke passed away in 1925, Doris's childhood was over. She was now the beneficiary of her father's unbreakable trust funds with an estimated $100 million and multiple homes across the country. Her father had given Doris some advice just before he died, which she turned into her motto: "Trust no one." Doris lived his words every day of her life. That is an almost unbearable situation for anyone, especially someone with $100 million and a few days shy of her thirteenth birthday. Image, for the rest of your life, trying to determine if everyone you meet is after you for your money.

Doris had to make that determination when she married her first husband James Cromwell, the son of a Palm Beach socialite, in 1935. She thought marriage would free her from her overbearing mother and at age twenty-three, she was ready to be on her own. Cromwell was more interested in New Deal politics than his young wife, and eventually he became ambassador to Canada. But Cromwell was more interested in using Doris's political connections than in keeping her satisfied. The couple also had one daughter, Arden, who lived exactly one day. Doris would never have another child. The couple divorced in 1943, and Doris went on to explore her sexuality. Doris had a string of famous lovers, including General George Patton, Olympic swimming champion and Hawaiian surfing legend Duke Kahanamoku and actor Errol Flynn. Flynn actually bragged to his friends he was sleeping with the richest girl in America and the richest boy in Sweden, apparently keeping them both happy for some time. Doris said her eyes were opened by her lover Duke Kahanamoku. She knew there must be someone more exciting in bed than her first husband James Cromwell.

In 1947, Doris would marry again, although love was certainly not the motivation for this marriage either. Her second husband was legendary playboy Porfirio Rubirosa, who was known for polo playing and bedding wealthy women. Doris actually purchased Rubirosa's services from a French socialite named Danielle Darrieux for the sum of $1 million. Rubirosa had a huge reputation as a legendary lover but also possessed somewhat of a shady past. Rubirosa was once employed as a hit man for Dominican leader General Trujillo, disguised under the job title of ambassador. He was also romantically linked to Marilyn Monroe, Ava Gardner, Zsa Zsa Gabor and was even married to the other gold dust twin, Barbara Hutton. Rubirosa's legendary sexual prowess came from his extremely large male genitalia. Let's just say it was so large, waiters in Newport referred to pepper mills as "rubirosas." Doris and Porfirio were only married a short time, but he was certainly well compensated for his time. He received a stable of polo ponies, luxury sports cars and a $3.5 million divorce settlement in 1951. The two remained friends and he was kept "on call" by an always-willing Doris Duke. To say she had a high sex drive would be an understatement.

Doris Duke and first husband James Cromwell (in light overcoat). Cromwell was more interested in his wife's political contacts than in keeping her satisfied. After the couple divorced in 1943, Doris would have a string of famous lovers, including General George Patton and Errol Flynn.

Doris's major attachment to Newport was her mansion on Bellevue Avenue, Rough Point, which her father had purchased in 1922. She started spending more time in her Newport manor after her mother's death in 1962. Doris would spend over half the year in her brownstone mansion overlooking the Atlantic Ocean. Doris also had a new personal attendant in her life. His name was Eduardo Tirella, a part-time actor and interior designer whom Doris had met through mutual friend Elizabeth Taylor. Tirella had reenergized Doris and was spending a lot of his time and her money turning the vast, empty and cold Rough Point into a warm and livable estate. Doris and Eduardo were inseparable. But like so many times previously in her life, she did not live in harmony for very long. Doris had learned Tirella was planning on leaving her and returning to Hollywood to become set designer for an upcoming Tony Curtis and Sharon Tate film called *Don't Make Waves*. Doris was devastated like a jilted lover. She begged and pleaded for Tirella to stay and promised that money was no object and that he could name his price. But Tirella had his heart set on returning to the West Coast and she could not stand in his way. Tirella would soon find out that when a person she trusted disappointed her, whether in business or between the sheets, he would be exiled from her inner circle forever.

Only Doris knew for sure the events that took place on the afternoon of October 7, 1966. Doris and Eduardo were leaving Rough Point around 3:00 p.m. to attend a meeting for the Preservation Society. Tirella was driving a rented station wagon and parked in front Rough Point's large wrought-iron gates. He then put the car in park and got out to swing open the heavy gates that guarded the grounds to the estate. Doris slid across to the driver's side to drive through the gates, then onto Bellevue Avenue. Then something happened. The car lurched forward, engine revving, and pinned the helpless Tirella against the impenetrable ironwork. The car continued forward, smashing through the gates, running over the helpless Tirella, dragging him under the car and then smashing into a tree across Bellevue Avenue. When the police arrived, they thought Doris was the only person involved in the incident. Only her incessant screaming, "Eduardo, where's Eduardo," prompted them to investigate further. Upon closer scrutiny, the police discovered bloodstains on the gate and street, small bits of brain matter and an eyeball. There was little left of Eduardo Tirella; the runaway car had ground him into bits. Doris was hysterical and spent the night sedated in the hospital.

When the police finally were able to interrogate Doris, she claimed their relationship was fine and that there was no disagreement between the two. But some eyewitnesses had claimed to see the couple arguing earlier in the day while antique shopping in downtown Newport. The pair had also been drinking heavily the night before while Doris was still trying to retain Eduardo's services and convince him to stay in her employ. There were also rumors that Doris had uncovered a homosexual affair Tirella was engaged in behind his mistress's back. Doris's explanation to the police was that the rental car's shifter confused her; she was not familiar with the push button operation and had mistakenly accelerated through the gate, killing her companion instantly. She told the police that the car just leaped forward and she couldn't remember anything after that. Newport Police Chief Joseph Radice ruled, in less than one week, that the incident was "an unfortunate accident" and no charges would be filed.

Did Doris murder her friend in a fit of jealous rage? If she did, she fooled the police and her vast wealth helped her get away with it. Chief Radice was forced to resign after a public outcry that he was too lenient and did not investigate the accident thoroughly. Public opinion was that Doris got away with murder. Apparently, a wealthy heiress was extremely generous to a former police chief in his retirement and all police records of the hasty investigation vanished. The Rough Point gates were freshly painted, the scrape marks were washed off the street and the rented station wagon disappeared forever. It was like the unfortunate accident never happened.

Doris Duke had deep pockets and lots of influential friends, especially in the police department.

Doris did something strange in 1968, just a few short years after her unfortunate accident; she founded the Newport Restoration Foundation as a way to preserve over eighty decaying colonial properties throughout the historic district in downtown Newport. Doris even created a beautiful colonial square below Trinity Church, dedicated as Queen Anne's Square during the bicentennial. Through her numerous political contacts, Doris arranged for Queen Elizabeth II to perform the dedication in person while visiting Boston for the 200th anniversary celebration of the United States. The royal yacht steamed south from Boston with the Queen aboard, but when she arrived in the square, Doris was nowhere to be found. Doris was not feeling well that day and did not attend. Queen Elizabeth quickly made her speech and boarded the yacht, angrily vowing never to return to Newport. The Queen was miffed that Doris Duke had snubbed her.

The Restoration Foundation was a welcome gesture for locals who wanted the numerous, run-down colonial homes preserved and restored to their eighteenth-century grandeur. Doris had also confided in friends that she was tired of seeing these run-down shacks on her way to and from Rough Point. A lot of people were skeptical and the timing seemed suspicious. Was Doris thanking the city of Newport for not looking too deeply into her "unfortunate

Although this area looks like an authentic colonial square, Queen Anne's Square was a creation of Doris Duke's Restoration Foundation. Doris used her political clout to bring Queen Elizabeth II to Newport to perform the dedication in 1976. *Photo courtesy of the author.*

accident"? If she was, she did it in the only way that she knew how to apologize: Doris opened her inexhaustible wallet. In Doris's world, money could fix anything.

Almost her entire life, fortune hunters, scam artists and bloodsuckers of every size and shape had stalked Doris Duke. Unfortunately, in 1985, a con artist slipped through Doris's usually impregnable defenses, and became a huge part of her life and what Doris would later call "the greatest mistake of my life." The wolf in sheep's clothing was named Chandi Heffner. Heffner was a flower child from Baltimore who had moved to Hawaii, had become a Hare Krishna and was watching Doris closely. Chandi had studied up on the wealthy heiress, learning her likes and dislikes, and discovered the death of her only child, Arden. Chandi finally conned her way into Doris's Hawaii mansion, Shangri-La, to reveal an interesting secret: Chandi Heffner was the reincarnation of her long dead daughter. Doris bought the scam hook, line and sinker. Doris was thrilled to have the mother-daughter relationship she had always craved. Chandi was soon running Doris's financial empire and injecting her with a concoction designed to improve her health and make her feel younger. To make the reunion official, Doris legally adopted Chandi and she became part of the family and legal heir to the Duke fortune. There were persistent rumors the adoption was just a coverup of their lesbian affair, although close friends disagreed. Doris was just happy to have a chance to be a mother, and besides, she loved men too much. Chandi would introduce another parasite into Doris's life. She brought in a new head butler named Bernard Lafferty. The gay, drunk, illiterate, ponytailed and often-barefoot Irish butler was now in charge of running the household staff. Chandi was now drunk with power and kept her new mom medicated as much as possible to run things as she saw fit.

Finally, in 1991, Doris had had enough. Through an examination by her personal physician, Doris learned she was slowly being poisoned by the so-called "health shots." When Doris learned of Chandi's plot to speed her demise and obtain her inheritance, Doris reacted like she always did when someone close to her became a nuisance or disappointment. Without telling Chandi, Doris fled Hawaii for one of her other estates and her newly adopted daughter was permanently denied entry into Shangri-La. Chandi was out of Doris's life, but by no means would it be the last time she would be heard from.

After Chandi's departure, Doris relied more and more on head butler Bernard Lafferty. Her health was steadily deteriorating, possibly from the cocktail of drugs her adopted daughter had been injecting into her veins. Doris confided in Lafferty that she was scared a Hare Krishna follower of Chandi's would murder her in her sleep. Lafferty fed the paranoia that

This trio was a strange combination of personalities. Doris Duke is on the left, exiled Philippine leader Imelda Marcos, center, and former Hare Krishna Chandi Heffner on the right. Heffner convinced Doris that she was the reincarnation of her stillborn baby.

Doris was feeling by agreeing with her assessment of the situation and made the fearful Doris even more anxious. But what Bernard Lafferty was really doing was turning Doris into more of a recluse, while he was her only contact with the outside world. Lafferty was increasing his power by transforming Doris into a prisoner in her own home. Doris Duke tried every possible treatment to stay young. In 1992, she was contemplating another face-lift and Bernard Lafferty was fervent and actually pressed Doris to go through with the procedure. Two days after the surgery, Doris fell and broke her hip. She was now 100 percent dependent on her head butler for just about everything. By early 1993, Bernard Lafferty was in complete control of Doris Duke's daily affairs and business operations. He was even given power of attorney for all of Doris's legal decisions. In February 1993, partially based on Bernard Lafferty's advice, Doris underwent double knee–replacement surgery, which is a risky surgery, especially for someone in her eighties. Doris had also suffered a series of recent strokes and her memory was hazy at best. She was becoming increasingly confused and disoriented. Concerned friends and relatives would call Falcon's Lair, Doris's Beverly

Hills mansion, to check on her health, only to be told by the Irish butler, "Miss Duke is fine, she is unable to come to the phone right now. I will tell her you called." None of the messages were ever relayed to the ailing heiress. Bernard Lafferty kept Doris in an almost constant drug haze while he lived the high life on her endless bankroll. He was constantly chauffeured to Los Angeles–area gay bathhouses and expensive shops along Rodeo Drive and even paraded around Falcon's Lair clad in her eveningwear.

The end would finally come on October 27, 1993, at 5:30 a.m. and Doris fought until the end. A physician was summoned to make her last hours on earth more comfortable and injected her with large amounts of Demerol and morphine. A nurse who witnessed the injections later testified that Doris was nowhere near death. Bernard Lafferty exercised his power of attorney to accelerate the inevitable. He knew what was contained in the final will. To lend some credibility to the nurse's claim, Lafferty had Doris's body cremated within two hours of her passing and no autopsy was ever performed. With the hasty cremation, Bernard Lafferty incinerated any possible evidence that he had heavily drugged his boss to get to his cut of the inheritance. Doris left strict orders in her will that after her death, her body was to be tossed into the Pacific Ocean so sharks could devour it, a ritual Doris had learned about in her many visits to Hawaii. She also requested that her eyes be donated to the New York eye bank. Both requests were quickly denied by the hurried incineration.

There was that one final matter of the will and, of course, with one of the world's largest personal fortunes up for grabs, the circus had just begun. Doris Duke was dead but the controversy was just beginning.

Doris's will was a complicated document, containing over forty pages of instructions on how the more than $1 billion estate was to be dispersed. The illiterate Irish butler was, incredibly, named executor, which included a $5 million payment, a $500,000 annual salary and complete control of how the money was to be allocated to charitable causes. Doris had requested the bulk of her liquid assets to be directed under an organization known as the Doris Duke Charitable Foundation. The money was supposed to fund art and theatrical programs and protect endangered wildlife as well as fund scientific research at Duke University. Her Newport mansion, Rough Point, was bequeathed to the Newport Restoration Foundation to be opened as a museum, and remains one today. Her pets were also well taken care of with sizeable inheritances. Her pet dog was gifted $100,000 and her two pet camels, Princess and Baby, which often roamed the grounds of Rough Point, were gifted money for their care as well. Doris had acquired the camels from a Saudi arms dealer when she was negotiating the purchase of a private jet. The Saudi businessman included them to entice Doris to complete the transaction. Doris also left strict instructions in the will that the $5 million she had loaned to exiled Philippine leader Imelda Marcos was to be repaid in full.

Many people wondered how a man who came directly from drug and alcohol rehab into Doris Duke's employ could wind up controlling a billion-dollar charitable organization. Now that he was fully in charge, Bernard Lafferty underwent a strange transformation. He dyed his hair blonde, cut off his trademark ponytail and lost a sizeable amount of his girth. It was almost like Bernard Lafferty was trying to become the living incarnation of his former boss, Doris Duke. He was still wearing her expensive gowns, lavishing himself with her jewels and spending the charity's money to excess. Lafferty was living the high life at Falcon's Lair, which ironically was the former estate of troubled Hollywood silent screen star Rudolph Valentino. Lafferty's excessive spending on illegal drugs, expensive brandy and designer clothes did not go unnoticed by the charity's trust company, which was in charge of overseeing the cash outflows. Lafferty's overindulgence got him removed as the will's executor for mismanagement. That did not stop his excessive partying and Lafferty would drink himself to the grave by 1996.

Another parasite who attached herself to the Duke fortune was con artist extraordinaire Chandi Heffner. Although Doris had strict instructions in her will that Chandi was not to be given a dime, as an adopted child, the law was on Heffner's side. The will stipulated the trust fund set up by Doris's father was to go to any living Duke heir. That included Chandi Heffner. The value of that trust fund had grown to $90 million, so the trust company now overseeing the management of Doris's fortune offered Chandi $65 million. She quickly accepted the cash and disappeared back to Hawaii.

The battle over the will was just the last sad chapter of a controversial and misunderstood life. Doris Duke was constantly searching for true love and probably never felt it after her beloved father passed away. Doris Duke should have had a wonderful life, surrounded by a loving family and close friends. Instead she had to constantly look over her shoulder and be suspicious of everyone she encountered to make sure they weren't out to get to her sizable fortune. Unfortunately, the never-ending parade of hucksters, con artists and pariahs were out for her money and were rarely looking out for Doris's best interests or well-being. Perhaps her life might have been simpler if she had just heeded her father's advice, "Trust no one!"

REVERSAL OF FORTUNE

For anyone who didn't know the intimate details of Sunny Crawford von Bülow's life, she seemed to have it all at first glance. She had inherited $75 million, had three bright and beautiful children and was once married to an Austrian prince. She was beautiful, often compared to a young Grace Kelly, and husband Claus seemed to dote on his attractive wife. Claus was a non-practicing attorney of German and Danish descent and had met his future wife while she was still married to her inattentive first husband, Prince Alfred of Auersperg. Sunny von Bülow lived in a world of privilege, with houses in both New York City and Newport. Staffs of servants waited on her every whim. But with all this affluence, Sunny was not happy. She was subject to bouts of depression that made her almost comatose and she frequently spoke openly about suicide. Things are not always as they appear. Sunny and Claus were at each other's throats. Claus was not happy living off of Sunny's fortune and wished to return to work. The couple also had an open marriage, and Claus was allowed to engage in any form of sexual behavior he wished, as long as the other participant was not part of their society circle. He broke this rule when, in 1979, Claus openly dated Alexandra Isles, the star of science-fiction soap opera *Dark Shadows*. A Newport property called Carey Mansion was used as the backdrop for this cult-favorite television series.

The events of December 21, 1980, at Sunny's Newport mansion, Clarendon Court, would put the small seaside town in the national media spotlight for years to come. That evening, Sunny was somewhat incoherent and was slurring her speech. Later in the evening, her son noticed Sunny was having a difficult time crawling into her bed. Claus was summoned from his study and assisted his wife into bed. Son Alexander was concerned his mother had taken an overdose of sleeping pills, which Sunny repeatedly denied. Her condition was dismissed as Sunny being overtired and it was believed a good night's sleep would return her to normal. The next morning, as the family gathered for breakfast around 11:00 a.m., Sunny was nowhere to be found, although this was not unusual. She was a late sleeper. Claus had arrived for breakfast around this time and had been awake since dawn, working in his study. He thought he had better check on his wife. When he walked into her bathroom, Claus discovered an alarming sight. Sunny was unconscious on the tile floor. She was also bleeding from the lip with her nightgown bunched around her waist and resting in a puddle of her own urine. Her body was ice-cold. An ambulance rushed Sunny to a Newport hospital where it was discovered her body temperature was eighty-one degrees. The local hospital was not able to handle this type of emergency properly so Sunny was transferred to a Boston trauma center. A CAT scan revealed the worst: Sunny's coma was irreversible.

That is when the whispers started, especially from Sunny's children from her first marriage: Claus was accused of trying to kill their mother for her money. Claus's indifference to Sunny's coma and insistence she be removed from life support did not look good for his innocence. His girlfriend Alexandra Isles also had expensive tastes and a $15 million inheritance share would certainly help to keep the mistress happy. The circumstantial evidence was beginning to mount against Claus and he was eventually indicted by a Rhode Island grand jury. Claus von Bülow would be tried for attempted murder. When Claus arrived at the Newport County Courthouse for his arraignment on July 13, 1981, there was a media circus awaiting his arrival. Every media outlet on the East Coast had a crew in Newport to cover the sensational attempted-murder trial. The trial of the century would finally begin in February of 1982. Over the next month, a parade of witnesses and family members would testify in the case. Von Bülow's defense case was based on a suicidal wife who wanted to die through a mix of drugs and alcohol. The prosecution focused on von Bülow's desire for his inheritance and a mysterious black bag containing syringes of insulin. The prosecution contended that von Bülow was injecting his wife with insulin to induce the coma. Apparently, the jury agreed with the prosecution and on March 16, 1982, he was found guilty on two counts of attempted murder. Von Bülow would later be sentenced to thirty years in prison.

Free on bail, Claus sought out famed Harvard law professor Alan Dershowitz to handle the appeal of the guilty verdicts. The Rhode Island Superior Court, in 1983, granted a new trial based on the evidence-gathering procedure in the first trial. It turned out a private detective hired by Sunny's children had discovered the mysterious black bag containing the suspected coma-inducing insulin. The private detective then turned over the damning evidence to law enforcement, which introduced it to evidence.

The von Bülow trial put Newport on the front page of national newspapers and was the lead story of nightly network newscasts. This is Claus von Bülow leaving a side entrance of the Newport County Courthouse. *Photo courtesy of the* Providence Journal.

The media circus follows the jury to visit the alleged attempted murder scene at Clarendon Court, the von Bülow's mansion on Bellevue Avenue. *Photo courtesy of the* Providence Journal.

Evidence-gathering protocol was not followed correctly and the evidence could have been planted or tampered with. When the new trial finally began, in April of 1985, the jury was not allowed to hear about the previously mentioned evidence contained in the illegally obtained black bag. Without this incriminating evidence, the prosecution had no direct evidence that Claus attempted to kill his socialite wife. It should be noted in Claus's defense that when a scientific analysis was conducted on the needle, there was no evidence of any of Sunny's blood or tissue. This seems to suggest that the evidence may have been planted to frame Claus for the attempted murder.

Apparently, the second jury felt the same way: Claus von Bülow was acquitted of all charges on June 10, 1985, and walked out of the Rhode Island Superior Courthouse a free man.

Attorney Alan Dershowitz wrote a book about his experience as Claus von Bülow's legal council called *Reversal of Fortune*. The book was made into a movie and Jeremy Irons, who portrayed Claus, won the Academy Award for Best Actor. Glenn Close did an admirable job representing the enigmatic Sunny.

Yet his not-guilty verdict did not satisfy Sunny's two children from her first marriage; they were convinced Claus was responsible for her irreversible coma. They even sued Claus to prevent him from any legal claims to Sunny's estate. Claus eventually signed documents that renounced all claims to his wife's millions in exchange for their daughter Cosima being reinstated as a beneficiary. Claus no longer felt comfortable living in the States and returned to London, where he writes theatre reviews.

Sunny's post-trial life would not turn out to be as pleasant. She lived in an irreversible vegetative state for many years at Columbia Presbyterian Hospital in New York City, requiring around-the-clock nursing care. Her hair and nails were still tended to on a regular basis; she ate via a feeding tube, but was still able to breathe on her own without the assistance of a respirator. Occasionally, her lips would curl into a wry smile and her eyes would open and tear up on rare occasions, especially during a visit from one of her children, but she would never utter another spoken word. Perhaps she was letting her loved ones know that she was finally at peace in her own little dream world, away from the bright lights and the pressures of high society. Sunny was recently moved to a private nursing facility and on December 6, 2008, she finally passed away, almost twenty-eight years to the day after she entered her coma. With her passing, she has likely taken the fateful events of December 21, 1980, to her grave, leaving friends and loved ones only to speculate about what actually transpired at the Newport estate.

Claus had no comment when asked about his ex-wife's death. He will have to live the rest of his days being pointed to as the man who caused Sunny's coma, even though he was found not guilty in a court of law. The court of public opinion can be a powerful sentence. Occasionally, people will refer to Claus as Dr. von Bulow. Claus will reply in his mocking and sarcastic tone, "One little injection and they make you a doctor."

Perhaps there is some truth behind Claus's derisive reply.

REFERENCES

Bart, Sheldon. *Beatrice: The Untold Story of a Legendary Woman of Mystery.* Newport, RI: Newport Legends, 1998.

Crane, Elaine Forman. *Killed Strangely: The Death of Rebecca Cornell.* Ithaca: Cornell University Press, 2002.

D'Agostino, Thomas. *Haunted Rhode Island.* Atglen, PA: Schiffer Publishing, 2005.

Dershowitz, Alan M. *Reversal of Fortune: Inside the Von Bülow Case.* New York: Random House, 1986.

Duke, Pony, and Jason Thomas. *Too Rich: The Family Secrets of Doris Duke.* New York: HarperCollins Publishers, 1995.

Eaton, John P., and Charles A. Haas. *Titanic: Triumph and Tragedy.* New York: W.W. Norton & Company, 1995.

Hoehling, A.A., and Mary Hoehling. *The Last Voyage of the Lusitania.* MD: Madison Books, 1956.

Kaplan, Justin. *When the Astors Owned New York: Blue Bloods and Grand Hotels in a Gilded Age.* New York: Viking Press, 2006.

Menzies, Gavin. *1421: The Year China Discovered America.* New York: HarperCollins Publishers, 2002.

Patterson, Jerry E. *First Four Hundred: New York and the Gilded Age.* New York: Rizzoli International Publications, 2002.

Renehan, Edward J., Jr. *Commodore: The Life of Cornelius Vanderbilt.* New York: Basic Books, 2007.

Stuart, Amanda Mackenzie. *Consuelo and Alva Vanderbilt.* New York: HarperCollins Publishers, 2005.

Vanderbilt, Arthur T., II. *Fortune's Children: The Fall of the House of Vanderbilt.* New York: William Morrow, 1989.

Printed in the USA
CPSIA information can be obtained
at www.ICGtesting.com
LVHW021730221123
764347LV00071B/932